GRANADA WINDOW

CLXX

Marguerite Steen has also written

Novels

    The Gilt Cage
    Duel in the Dark
    The Reluctant Madonna
    They That Go Down
    When the Wind Blows
    Unicorn
    Stallion
    The Wise and the Foolish Virgins
    Spider
    Matador
    The One-Eyed Moon } Spanish Trilogy
    The Tavern
    Return of a Heroine
    Who Would Have Daughters?
    The Marriage Will Not Take Place
    Family Ties
    The Sun is My Undoing
    Rose Timson
    Twilight on the Floods. (In preparation)
    Phoenix Rising. (In preparation)

Short Stories

    A Kind of Insolence.

Biography

    The Lost One: Mrs. Perdita Robinson
    Hugh Walpole
    William Nicholson

Plays

    Matador. (With Matheson Lang)
    French for Love. (With Derek Patmore)
    Oakfield Plays. (For Children)
    Peepshow: a Children's book of theatrical
                            production

GRANADA WINDOW

by Sir William Nicholson

GRANADA WINDOW

by

Marguerite Steen

London
THE FALCON PRESS

First published in 1949
by The Falcon Press (London) Limited
*7 Crown Passage, Pall Mall, London, S.W.*1
Printed in Great Britain
by Willmer Bros. & Company Ltd.
Birkenhead

AUSTRALIA
The Invincible Press,
Sydney, Melbourne, Brisbane, Adelaide.
NEW ZEALAND
The Invincible Press, Wellington
SOUTH AFRICA
M. Darling (Pty.) Ltd., Capetown

HOMAJE

al

EXMO. SR. DUQUE DE ALBA

The frontispiece is reproduced from a painting by Sir William Nicholson, and the endpaper and the illustration facing page 16 *are reproduced from drawings by Gregorio Prieto.*

CONTENTS

CHAPTER I

SPANISH HERO

Happy the reader who makes his first acquaintance of the immortal history of Don Quijote de la Mancha in the country which gave it birth.

The right way, but it is not open to everyone, must be to walk, with the old volumes of the original under one's arm, or in one's knapsack, away into the country: to sit down near some little threshing-floor or in the shadows of an olive grove: to read a little, blinking in the sun: to eat one's meal of bread and olives and cheese, to wash it down with red wine of the country, and to read a little more, before dropping asleep. It is more than likely that Sancho Panza himself will wake you with a courteous greeting, and that you will meet three of four lean, ragged Don Quijotes, on their unspeakable Rozinantes, who will send you with God on your journey home.

You will certainly, on your decent, unhurried journey, meet Don Quijote and many Sanchos Panzas; it may be you will also meet someone whom you take for Don Juan Tenorio. But you will be wrong; Don Juan burns eternally in hell fire, and that which you see is only the ruddy glow from its furnaces which illuminates the face of an ardent disciple. You will be lightly told that 'every Andalucian is a Don Juan', but I shall hope presently to show you why this is only a piece of innocent boasting, in which the soul of the Andalucian delights: one of the picturesque lies which are blown like froth about the surface of a friendly conversation.

The peculiar pleasure of reading *Don Quijote* lies partly in the fact that today, in the country districts, the peasants are living the same lives that they lived when Cervantes was writing his epic—of which Maeztu speaks somewhere as 'Spain laughing at itself so that it should not weep'. They are eating the self-same food, sleeping in similar houses—indeed, in some cases, in the identical houses, they are washing their clothes in the same streams, their donkeys are carrying the same loads, of brushwood for bedding, of bread and vegetables and fuel from door to door. Their houses still consist, in many instances, of a single room, with, perhaps, a loft above it, with a great square door that seems to belong to a barn or coach house, with a fireplace but no chimney, so that the smoke of the olive wood branches fills the room with its sweet, stifling scent. Their windows are still unglazed, and the shutters with which they exclude the piercing cold of winter are bleached silver with the same sun. They still warm themselves at braziers, they don in cold weather the shabby descendants of the same noble cape which Cervantes must have slung across his shoulders as he butted his way through the slicing wind that sweeps the Castillan plateau to the Madrid tavern where he wrote most of his chapters. The shepherds wear the same coats of sheepskin and the same sandals thonged across their feet burnt black in the sun, and in a few regions of the *sierras* the brigands still ride their horses up craggy hillsides that one would think would defeat a goat. Their amusements are still the same: telling stories, singing, dancing and drinking the wine whose blessing they rank with the sun's.

And because they have been doing these self-same things for centuries, and because, in the lovely wild country places where one can count the visible dwellings upon the fingers of a single hand, or, more probably, may search for them in vain, they have not encountered the corrupting influences of the towns, each simple act and word has become invested with a significance out of all proportion with its actual meaning. They themselves are tradition made flesh, and to know Don Quijote one must know them, in the same way that knowledge of them will shed light upon many of the long, slow, winding paragraphs of Don Quijote.

Like Sancho Panza, they are compounded of crude superstition, natural sceptical common-sense and pure ignorance, mingled with a graceful reverence for anyone whose intellectual parts are greater than their own. A writer, to them, is like a god.

Unless you know something of Don Quijote de la Mancha and Don Juan Tenorio, your knowledge of the people among whom you are wandering will be incomplete, and you are likely to jump to many false conclusions. These two characters summarize so much of the national temperament that, by studying them, it is possible to arrive at a very fair understanding of the people as a whole. The danger of studying them apart from their natural environment lies in the fact that one is apt to colour them with one's own national point of view and prejudice, so that, very easily, in the long run, one's study may amount to nothing.

Still, if one can manage to keep one's mind perfectly clear and pure: if, above all, one can sink that fatal British inclination—which, in the case of Don Juan, is worse than fatal—to look for blacks and whites, for moral values and sentimental undertones, one will surely gain something that will illuminate one's outlook upon this (from a British point of view) curiously alien, but profoundly fascinating people.

Let us remember that there does not exist a more cold-bloodedly practical being than the Spaniard; that his romanticism has been invented for him by the foreigner; that he is the greatest realist in the world, a natural cynic, and that the entire range of Spanish imaginative art and literature is built upon practical premises, upon action rather than dream. Cynicism, irony, the grotesque: these are what arouse the laughter of the Spaniard, and they are not in the equipment of the romantic; they alarm him, they make him curl up into himself. Parody is the Spaniard's supreme delight, and Cervantes, having given the world the parody of all time, in *Don Quijote*, is his idol. Another aspect of his idolatry embraces the monastic figure of Frey Gabriel Tellez, who, using the pseudonym of Tirso de Molina, gained his literary laurels by creating, in *El Burlador de Sevilla*, the character of Don Juan Tenorio, in whom he crystallizes a certain stone-cold, non-moral valour which one meets, perhaps, most nearly, in some of the modern bull-fighters, and which, to a great part of the Spanish public, represents the apogee of the heroic.

I was much entertained in the course of my enquiry into the history and antecedents of the imaginary person whom I have christened Spanish Hero to come across a scrap of information whose modern flavour delighted me with its relevance to our subject.

I am enchanted to discover that during the seventeenth century, domestic, scholastic and ecclesiastical circles were plunged into a ferment by the stubborn preference expressed by young Juan and young Juanita for certain volumes, strongly disapproved by their parents and spiritual guardians which seem to have been the very forefathers of our modern novels: garnishing the dull dish of history with amorous and voluptuous descriptions that were supposed to be highly imflammatory to youthful senses.

Up to the time of Cervantes, since the wars of Carlos V, Spanish writers had confined themselves to translating *The Decameron*, and to imitating, not very brilliantly, the style of Boccaccio. From these imitations sprang the so-called literature of chivalry which, according to the preface to the 1735 translation, 'degraded the spirit and corrupted the morals of Christendom'. It is not quite what one associates with the name of chivalry, which, however, like other words in the English language, has evidently gathered a coat of whitewash in passing down the ages.

This literature of chivalry, *libros de caballería*, was a natural development of the age—an age of crusade, of banditti, of battle, of prolonged historic warfare against the Moors in the south—into whose records the gleeful but unscrupulous historian wove as much fable of giants, monsters, enchantments and marvels as he felt his readers would swallow—and, to do him justice, their taste was insatiable—and into which, with the advance of Christianity, a new and exciting idea of gallantry now started to percolate.

Woman as the domestic beast suddenly made way for woman as the romantic inspiration. Knighthood lost its *raison d'être* as mere proof of physical valour, and the fatal introduction of what old-fashioned writers call 'the fair sex' into a setting heretofore exclusively masculine set an entirely new standard of performance and award.

According to another preface, this time in 1842, 'This immoderate taste for the chivalric literature soon bore its fruits. Young persons, estranged from the study of history, which did not satisfy their ill-regulated curiosity, took the books of their choice. Obedience to the caprice of women, adulterous amours, false points of honour, sanguinary vengeance for the most trivial injuries, unbridled luxury, contempt for social order, all these were brought into practice, and books of chivalry thus became not less fatal to good manners than to good taste.'

It was these opinions, with their curiously nonconformist flavour, that gave Cervantes his inspiration for Don Quijote.

What manner of man was this Cervantes? In *Don Quijote* you may find the answer to the question, for the two interpret one another, and no historical record can tell you more than may be learnt in the perusal of its pages.

Such meagre information as one can gather about this illustrious writer, who paid for the tardy honours of posthumous fame by a lifetime of suffering and privation, is easily available, for I have not come across an edition which does not print some version of its author's life among the prefatory matter.

To summarize it briefly—Madrid, Sevilla, Toledo, Lucena, Esquivias, Alcazar de San Juan and Consuegra fought out, over a long term of years, their individual claims to having cradled the genius: until the discovery of his birth certificate in the church of Santa María at Alcala de Henares settled it once and for all. His tomb is equally obscure for, dying upon the same date according to the Gregorian calendar as Shakespeare, Saturday, April 23rd, 1616, he left instructions that he should be buried in the convent of the Trinitarians which, a little before, had received his natural daughter, Doña Isabel de Saavedra. But in the year 1633, the convent was moved from the calle del Humilladero to the calle de Cantaranas, and it is not known what became of the ashes of Cervantes, of which no tomb, no stone, no inscription marks the resting-place: a tragically fitting end for one whose life was tuned to humiliation and passed against a background of poverty.

His struggling, studious youth, his enlistment under Don Juan of Austria, his valiant conduct and the wounds he received in the battle of Lepanto, his capture by Barbary corsairs, his ransom, and his romantic love-affair with a Portuguese lady of high rank, by whom he had his daughter, Doña Isabel, form a chivalric tapestry as rich as any woven by the old romancers.

The magnificent recompense of his valour and talents was his appointment as clerk to a victualling board, during which appointment he was accused of malversation of public monies, and flung into prison until he had proved his innocence. Broken in health, and almost wholly without means, he took to poetry as a profession, supplementing his literary earnings by acting as agent in various business negotiations, and by writing dramas for the theatre.

At the age of fifty, in a mood of profound sadness and discouragement, he conceived and wrote his tragic master-piece, but lacking the influential patronage necessary (even in present-day Spain) to bring genius to public notice, he gained little thereby. Spain laughed; but there were too few serious and thoughtful people to penetrate the light, ironic surface of the book into its dark and melancholy depths. Pursued by want, forgotten by many, unknown to all, Miguel de Cervantes Saavedra died in solitude and poverty, and two centuries went by before his admirers thought fit to adorn with a little medallion the last house in which he lived, and to rename in his honour a little side-street in Madrid.

Díaz de Benjeuma writes:

'The reader must meditate upon the series of so rapid successes, so great and so extraordinary, which filled the period of Cervantes' youth: which needed no more than a simple setting forth to form a dramatic framework, an absorbing poem in themselves. For what was the foundation, what the motive power, what the first and last of all his actions?—The man of powerful soul, struggling against spiritual and material adversity.

'And what is the story of Don Quijote but the allegory of similar successes? Here is the physically weak man, of great spiritual strength, struggling against obstacles which are opposed to the common happiness of the human race.'

Struggling and failing, Benjeuma should have said: for it is the failures which lend the book its immortal humanity.

Cervantes himself possessed an enormous library of these old *libros de caballería;* knew and loved them, and, as a young man, had gone out of his way to put their ideas into practice. When experience and advancing years showed him their futility, he devoted himself to this tragic parody, which captured the public taste already sated with heroics and in a mood to respond to his challenge. For the Spanish temperament, which does not, like the French, kindle to facile jesting, is instantly stirred by the profound and subtle humour of parody.

Ivan Turgénev says of *Don Quijote:* 'It is the symbol of faith', contrasting it with the other immortal work, published in the same year, Shakespeare's *Hamlet,* which he calls 'the symbol of doubt'. Don Quijote is the idealist who acts, and Hamlet the idealist who thinks and analyses. It is probably because Turgénev himself belongs to the Hamlet class that he so adores Don Quijote. In one is developed a study of sensuality and egoism which, slowly overwhelming a character apparently good and heroic, finally destroys it; while, no matter how shadowed by his madness, his follies, his ridiculous adventures and windy speechmaking, the supreme goodness of Don Quijote always triumphs.

It is, on the face of it, a very simple story, of an imaginary hero who, acting upon a chivalrous impulse, persuades a peasant to accompany him on a journey, to realize the Good of the earth. It has none of the forced allegorical flavour that makes Bunyan unreadable to the majority; the heavy-handed script of the lay preacher has nothing in common with the delicate flourish of genius which graces every line of the Spanish classic.

One needs, I think, to lay aside all the pretentious twaddle that has grown up, as it grows up around any masterpiece—about its being a system of philosophy, a programme of government, a theological synthesis and heaven knows what beside—because that is enough to scare away any unsophisticated reader, and one cannot afford to be scared away by Don Quijote. Let us think of it as lightly as Cervantes thought of it when, pen in hand and wine-bottle at elbow, he sat down to liberate that laughter enbalmed in tears which his own experience had brought him.

He had to begin with, no distinct design, beyond that of grouping some ludicrous adventures round a madman and a dolt, such as would display in their most extravagant light the follies of so-called chivalry. That this was his definite intent is shown in his preface, which names the book 'an invective against the books of chivalry, which sort of books Aristotle never dreamed of, Saint Basil never mentioned, nor Cicero once heard of'.

But the man's natural nobility defeated his original purpose, as he gradually made the discovery, in the act of writing, not that he was growing to love, but that he had always loved, his hero. The importance and gravity of his work, started in a mood of flippancy, takes hold on him: mockery dies. His characters, originally mere pegs for his ironic fancy, become in his own words, 'the children of his understanding'.

Don Quijote, the fool, the madman, the midnight watcher of broken armour, the murderer of sheep, the tilter at windmills, becomes the good man in revolt at injustice, whose dream is to make himself the comforter of the afflicted, the supporter of the weak, the bane of the proud and wicked; and Sancho Panza, originally the clown, the dolt, develops a sly subtlety, a limited but unerring good sense, a natural clearness of perception which, had his poor master but the wit to trust to it, might save many of them an awkward moment.

We see these two men becoming each other's second self bound in a touching loyalty, in an unanimity of valorou impulse which destroys the reader's mockery. Always the butt of the spectators, performing incredibly foolish things and suffering their consequences, the one upheld by his dream and the other by his obstinacy—they affect as much

GREGORIO PRIETO. 1934.

as they amuse. As characters they are individually lovable, and as types, using the very language, the very symbols which are current today, they embody the eternal sentiments of the Spanish race.

In the second part of *Don Quijote*, which was not written until ten years after the first part had appeared, Cervantes discards the thin chivalric thread upon which the adventures of Part One are strung, and offers an instance almost unique in the annals of literature—of a second part which, written as an after-thought, not merely equals but surpasses the first. It is this second part which gives *Don Quijote* the immortality which, as a mere satire, it would not have achieved; and it is to the second part that I recommend those who wish to know the real nobility, the real heroism, and the profound wisdom of Cervantes.

If its original success was due to its appeal to the sense of the ludicrous, its enduring fame rests upon its world-wide philosophy, its brave parables, its mild and illuminating criticism of human nature in general. Its appeal to his own period consisted in the contrast of the prosaic with the poetic, the constant triumph of the former, and the long overdue conclusion which every thoughtful Spaniard had reached in his own mind: that true heroism and chivalry do not consist in the pursuit of some extravagant and exceptional line of conduct which had come to be vulgarly considered as chivalric; and that the most innocent and well-disposed of human beings, if he insist upon following such a line, can become nothing but a laughing-stock for the world.

Cervantes let in light and air upon the corrupt and diseased thing which, thriving in darkness, had inflamed and strangled the will power and moral judgment of his contemporaries, and did this in no savage, Savonarolean spirit of purgation, but lightly, accidentally, almost, with a tragic delicacy that set them laughing at themselves for fear, as Maeztu says, they should weep.

Now, Don Juan is a more difficult pill for the Nordic to swallow. One must, however, study him if one is to complete the Spanish picture: if not in anticipation of meeting his prototype, for the light which the Don Juan cult throws upon the picture as a whole.

One must, in studying Don Juan, if one is to make a true and dispassionate estimate of his heroic value, throw away all the Good-Bad conventions, and judge him purely upon his personality and the sum of his achievements. Again, Maeztu:

'They don't know our Don Juan, el Burlador, and I think if they did their first impulse would be to deport him for an undesirable alien.'

He goes on to say, very truly, that everyone talks about Don Juan in the north, but that no one understands him: that every writer has studied him, but that none has written anything of importance about him. Which indeed is true, for it is part of the Nordic cult not to take Don Juan seriously.

Probably very few people beyond students have read the dramatic poem, *El Burlador de Sevilla*—the Jester of Sevilla. It is certainly not generally available outside of Spain, and although there must be translations, I myself have never come across an English one. Merely on hearsay, Don Juan has gained 'a certain reputation' which, although not wholly inaccurate in its outlines, does him very much less than justice.

To begin with, the inveterate and, if I may say so, tedious sentimentality of the North has turned him into the 'Great Lover', wandering in search of the ideal woman, burdened with a love he finds it difficult to dispose of, because all the women to whom he offers it seem to be slightly shocked by his advances. Such a conception is worse than ridiculous; it is an affront to Spanish psychology, and it staggers any Spaniard to whom one may present it. According to his own countrymen, the man who seeks an ideal woman is not a soul over-burdened with love, but a romantic egoist. If Don Juan were as burdened by love as the North makes out, his disillusionments would be in proportion to his deceptions. But Don Juan never knows disillusionment, because he is far too intelligent to have illusions. Herein lies the whole force, strength and resilience of his characters: which is granted him by the Spaniard who, according to one of his own writers, knows that ideals are not necessary, having lived three hundred years without them!

Let us briefly summarize what the name of Don Juan stands for in English opinion: libertinage, betrayal, lack of principle, swashbucklering, ostentation. It is characteristic of us as a nation, that swooping upon his less savoury characteristics, we overlook that which constitutes his first claim to importance: his immaculate courage, which is the greater since, contrary to Molière's Don Juan, Molina's is not an atheist, and not a blasphemer, and does believe in the after-life. It is just another instance of Henry VIII and Charles II, whose glories are foreshortened in public memory because each had the indiscretion to give free rein to that healthy gusto for feminine society which in England is considered reprehensible, in Spain is natural and normal.

I do not for a moment pretend that Don Juan can proffer a claim to public regard that compares in any way with that of these two kings; he was, indeed, a rowdy, precocious and libertine youth, an artist in the provocation and seduction of women, callous to the last degree in his rejection of an outworn pleasure, a stranger to the truth and a sybarite in his love for sumptuous living, rich clothes, a luxurious table and nights of rapture. That is how the monk Tirso de Molina conceived him and how Zorilla left him. 'A brute force, instinctive, petulant, but inexhaustible, triumphant and overwhelming; the symbol of an unquiet Spain, which accepts its courage for law and its will for royal edict.'

Love, for Don Juan, is a battle in which there is no pity for the vanquished. His methods could not be more clownish; he has no subtlety, although a degree of cunning, which prompts him, in the society of ladies of high rank, to trust to his animal attraction, rather than his power of enthralling them with his social graces. With the duquesa Isabela and Doña Iñez de Ulloa, he carries out his fell design under the dark and silent cloak of night. If he courts little waiting-maids, like Tisbea and Aminta, he promises them matrimony, and does not forget to mention the fact that he is a very influential young man of high position.

'I am a gentleman-in-waiting of the Ambassador of Spain,' says he; and—'My father is a justice of the peace and in the confidence of the king.' These plain excerpts are surely enough to explode the 'Great Lover' fallacy by which northern Europe tries to excuse its dalliance with so dubious a hero as Don Juan. In this aspect he is simply the sublime cad, with the courage of his convictions: which are that the world is his oyster-bed, and each pearl dedicated to his hand should he deign to gather it.

This, however, is only one side of the medal, the more showy, better-known one, which the Spaniard passes over or accepts with a laugh. The Spaniard does not, as we do, confuse a man's private life, or his amatory exploits, with his general moral worth.

Don Juan's sensuality saves him from the cold horror of diabolism which, lacking it, he might attain to; for his other aspect, which we are about to consider, is a formidable one: it is the one which, in conjunction with his libertinage, gives him his hold upon the Spanish imagination.

In Galicia and other provinces, the custom prevailed during the sixteenth century and the beginning of the seventeenth, of celebrating the feasts of the dead on the night of the second of November, with noisy orgies in the churches, altars laid out with cups and platters, and a profusion of meats and wines. This custom survives, in isolated parts of the country, in little offerings of food, laid by the peasants on the graves of their relatives.

As the wine-fumes mounted to the heads of the company, they began to offer sacrilegious toasts to the dead, who lay in the stone archways and vaults of the adjoining chapels, and imagination, kindled by the potent libations, soon conjured up the vision of the dead, themselves holding a banquet in rivalry with the banquet of the living—the sounds of whose macabre jesting reached the living ears, and sometimes drove more sensitive hearers out of their minds.

This situation was frequently exploited in the works of contemporary poets and singers, and with many variations. I have come on an interesting old version in which a young man, going to church not to hear the mass but to gloat on the pretty women, kicks a skull out of the way. Later, when he is supping with a friend, he receives, through a page-boy, a mysterious summons; he finds it is the skull, come to bid him sup with it in its tomb. He goes, out of bravado: there is a lovely descriptive passage that tells of the cocks crowing in the darkness as he passes, in which one senses a reference to the betrayal of Christ. The skull is very kind to the young man, however, and apart from frightening him out of his wits, imposes no more awful punishment upon him than to say a prayer whenever he sees a skull lying by the wayside.

This poem is sixteenth century, but the versions persist, and grow rather more ribald, into the present day. The Spanish love a grim subject, which they handle with a dry lightness which from our point of view adds horror to it, but which is the perfectly sincere expression of their natural cynicism.

Tirso de Molina had the idea of adding this excellent legend to his original concept of Don Juan, and if one only takes into account the Sublime Cad aspect, and ignores the valour of Don Juan, who attends the ghastly banquet with the Stone Commander, one knows only half of his character, and that the less important half. It is the union of the two, in Molina's narrative, which lends Don Juan Tenorio the peculiar fascination which he exercised upon the seventeenth-century public and which survives today. In the modern Spaniard's adoration of valour we may trace the survival of the old chivalric ideal; it is the motive that supports the bull-fight and glorifies the matador, it is the living flame which animates the moribund carcase of the old Spain, and which, like the rainbow in the sky, is the holy sign that Spain shall never be destroyed.

Tirso de Molina gave him a grand, sulphuric and unregenerate end; in the original version Don Juan goes to eternal damnation, played about by clear, bright lightning. This is the most artistic, as well as the most honourable finish for one whose greatest honour lay in his unrepentant roguery. But the writer Zorilla, who, taking Molina as a pattern, wrote another version of Don Juan, in the attempt to make him more human loaded him with an obscure, unconvincing Christian conversion, and an ascent to heaven in the midst of pink clouds and unsexed angels—surely an insult to the pride and insolence of the man. Besides being artistically indecent, this strikes one as a sheer destructive perversion of the character. We are at a loss to know what prompted it, because the Spaniard does not, as a general rule, make artistic mistakes, and having perpetrated a dubious action, it is not his way to repent of it in public, although he may interview his confessor very hurriedly and pay the usual penance as quickly as possible. But evidently Zorilla became queasy over his Don Juan, and, having enormously enjoyed tracing his unregenerate career, thought it better to put himself and his creation on the side of the angels as a finishing touch.

It is because I am convinced that Molina's Don Juan is the real Don Juan that I said a little earlier that one is not likely to meet Don Juan today. There is more than a touch of the superhuman in his lofty callousness, and it is his indifference to the after-life, combined with his belief in it, which emphasizes his superhumanity. It is easy to be valiant if one is, like many young Spaniards of today, an atheist; it is altogether different if one believes in hell and purgatory and the doctrines of retribution.

That is why I say that the matador who faces the bull in the ring, although possessed of Don Juan's cold, unimaginative courage (and there are one or two like this, although there are more who visualize only too clearly the meaning of the first slip, the first miscalculation), and who conquers women as he conquers his bulls, is not quite Don Juan: because, although he faces death nobly, by his own free will, and with full knowledge of all that awaits him before he attains the holy mystery of paradise, there is not, I think, a matador in all Spain who, before going into the ring, has not knelt in the little chapel of the bullring to place himself under the protection of the Christ of Great Power and of the Virgin

For much of the material in this article, which was first given as a lecture to the Bradford Literary & Philosophical Society, I wish to acknowledge my indebtedness to *Don Quijote, Don Juan y la Celestina*, by Ramiro de Maeztu.

CHAPTER II

PANORAMA I

IF, now and again, I speak of Granada as though it were Andalucía, and of Andalucía as though it were Granada, I hope I may be forgiven by those qualified to point out the inaccuracy of my statements. For, of course, Granada is not Andalucía; there is actually, in its spiritual and temperamental make-up, so little that is Andalucían, in the sense that Sevilla is Andalucían, that visitors in search of the shining white, orange-laden south, of the *juerga* and the *romeria*, are to be excused if, after their perfunctory exploration of the Alhambra and the Generalife, they hasten on to their next calling-place: a little discomposed by a town which, unlike most of the southern tourist centres, does little or nothing to detain or beguile the stranger.

Yet of all Andalucía that I travelled, in my one and only attempt at *turismo*, Granada was the town that reached out to me: that took and held me, saying, 'This, whether you like it or not, is your destiny; you can no more escape it or forget it than you can cancel out time.'

I have—let's admit it—no gift for *turismo*. In visiting a new country, my first preoccupations are with the people and with the landscape; only when I feel that my contacts with these are established can I be troubled with the architecture, with the arts, with the occupations—which interest me far more as revelation of local and national character than as historical, artistic or industrial units.

The people, the soil; the soil, the people. If one manages to know these, does not the rest explain itself? And in what country can one find this theory of mine more clearly exploited than in Spain, where the relation between the soil and the people who live upon it, drawing from it their personal characteristics of bitter, of sweet, of endurance and energy or of lassitude, can be marked and contrasted from province to province?

The savage individuality of the Spanish earth is the individuality of its people; the heat and cold of its climate are equally reflected in their chalerous emotions and the ice-cold rationalism of their intellectual outlook. The nearer the soil, the truer the character; and perhaps this explains why I have always, in Spain, sought the company of very simple people in preference to that of those who have sacrificed some of their national integrity to the extraneous influences that are found in densely populated areas: to foreign habits of thought, to sophisticated opinions, and to that superficial type of culture that leads away from one's true axis of existence without attaching one securely to another.

The landworkers, the small tradesfolk, the stockbreeders, the bullfighters, the tavern-keepers—these are the people who speak with the authentic voice of Spain. It is not, perhaps, a voice of the highest intelligence; it is seldom discreet, but it is painfully sincere, and expresses, often, a grievance. It is acutely conscious that it is drowned in the bellow of a thousand others, belonging to people who have their own axes to grind, to corrupt politicians, to systems of civic government that operate in favour of the rich, and seldom of the poor—yet it is not embittered. It has the dying fall of an infinite philosophy, and its burthen, at least in Andalucía, is apt still to be—'There is always the sun on the wall.'

How I have wished I had the combined strength and energy to tramp through Andalucía! Unhappily, I am one of those wretches whose feet, apparently, were never intended to serve any more useful purpose than to provide pegs for the shoe-designer's fancy; and on that first visit I was very tired, and in search only of a place to rest in. It was this that made me buy a book of those obliging kilomotric tickets which enable one to wander round and round Andalucía, practically without let or hindrance, when artfully employed in connection with a few motor 'buses, or—in extravagant and exhausted moments—the hired car.

Here let me say that motoring in Andalucía (or indeed in almost any part of Spain) calls for cast-iron nerves and a childlike faith in the driver who, while taking you round a hairpin bend at 80 k.p.h., with a drop of four hundred feet on the offside, will certainly turn to yell at you some poignant detail about a fatal accident which occurred on this very spot only two days ago. You must harden yourself to looking down some dizzy chasm upon the wreckage of a lorry or private car, as you must harden yourself to the fact that, on a long autobus journey, three-quarters of your companions will be violently sick while the rest groan, pillow their heads and consume quantities of cold *tortilla* (a kind of leathery omelette) in the apparent hope of inducing sickness.

Taking one thing with another, I prefer, and have even grown to love, the long, slow journeys by train, across plains on which the swathes of iris are flung like long blue scarves, through the tossed regions of the olivares, where the long groves of the trees are drawn in pewter-coloured ribbons across the red earth, and in the shadows of the angry purple and garnet *sierras*, whose towering escarpments reduce to insignificance the human life that goes on about their feet.

I love the dawdling pace of the train, its long, irrational pauses, which always seem to occur in some place where the panorama is of an almost intolerable splendour. I have often contrasted this pleasant habit of Spanish trains, of lingering in lovely places, with the almost invariable custom, in England, of drawing up between a row of derelict trucks and a clump of gasometers. I wonder whether the engine-driver himself has surrendered to the spectacle, and is leaning on the rail of his little cabin, lost in the infinite. This would not be at all out of the Andalucían character; the guard, who is sure at some stage of the journey to come into your compartment to smoke a friendly cigarette and to discuss the prospects of *los toros*, will, at the height of his peroration on Ortega, or Armillita, or Lalanda, break off to rhapsodize on the glories of the landscape.

The main difference between Spanish and English railroad travel seems to be that, in England, from the start, everyone is chafing to 'get there', whereas in Spain, no one ever expects to get there at all, and arrival at one's destination comes in the nature of a pleasant surprise, involving farewells to friends made on the journey, a final chat with the guard—who probably entrusts you with messages to members of his family, who happen to live in the town at which you have arrived—a casual assembly of personal effects, and a gentle, indeterminate amble towards the cab, car, taxi or whatever may be waiting at the entrance to the station.

The thing which must inevitably strike the traveller who visits Spain for the first time is the manner in which her landscape has been traduced, not only by foreign but by indigenous painters. The poster-like effects, those vulgar combinations of screaming blues, oranges and magentas— nothing can give a more lying impression of the pale, flakey and brittle brilliance of the scene, the delicate chalkiness that reaches its climax at midsummer: so that, looking upon it from afar, one receives almost the same sensual impression as that got from the window of a beauty parlour—where all the little cones of different coloured face powders, rose, saffron, lilac and green, invite one to press one's fingers into the soft, dry, resistless mass. I have often felt, looking across those summer plains, as though, by pressing my finger on some rosy hill, some pearl-coloured village, these would disintegrate, leaving nothing but a trace of silvery ash clinging to a finger-nail.

The only positive colour in Spain is in its skies and its shadows; the earth serves but to reflect that resplendent light, that drains all of its richness to ghostly rose, ghostly amber, on which the shadows, with their underlying richness of umber and orange, lie with more solidity than the objects which fling them.

How much of the travel-agency Spain does one realize on one's first visit to Andalucía? Probably a good deal, if one is content to follow the beaten paths, to trail like a good little performing animal in the wake of the guide who conscientiously insists upon showing off all those aspects of the town or countryside which form the spectacular nucleus of that which is supposed to appeal to the tourist. The natives will contribute their share, for it is in the Andalucían temperament to dramatize itself, as it is in the Andalucían temperament to hold passionately by tradition, and to love with an intensely personal devotion the soil on which it breeds.

But, unless it is *feria* time, or a day of *corrida*, you will see no shawls or mantillas. The elderly women, and the more sedate younger ones, still wear the *velo*, the frail piece of black lace that protects their tight marcel waves, their too-often peroxided curls from the sun. Alas, yes, young Andalucía is going blonde; the pale yellow locks frame uneasily the lovely olive complexions, or are allied to thick layers of pink and white maquillage, from which black velvety eyes and exquisite dark brows stare with mask-like effect. The ultra moderns have deserted the *velo* for Madrid versions of Paris fashions, which they poise consciously, and, it must be admitted, not yet very successfully, on their pretty heads.

It is unusual to meet a Spanish girl in her 'teens who is not lovely; in the early twenties the loveliness has begun to fade, and by the time she reaches the thirties its last traces have vanished in the fat which comes from physical indolence, excessive eating and the continuous nibbling of sweetstuffs and chocolates. The only Andalucían women who are beautiful in their middle age are the gipsies, the hardships of whose lives fine down the flesh and strengthen the traits of character in their hard, handsome faces.

The men, on the other hand, are very striking; their bearing is magnificent, to the last degree conscious, their manners superb. There is, perhaps, no more impressive sight than the Andalucían gentleman, in his immaculate black broadcloth, the coat cut rather low to reveal the pleated cambric shirt on whose left breast is embroidered the wearer's monogram, and his black Cordobés hat worn always at an angle. Such refinement of foppery, however, is left to the elderly; the Andalucían youth chooses rather to electrify the eye with American-style suits of a lilacy grey, of bright, vicious purple or, even more sensational, of a light peacock blue. The trousers are cut in an exaggeration of the so-called 'Oxford bags', the shoulders padded out to an aggressive squareness. This masterpiece of unfortunate taste is usually combined with a Cordobés hat of the palest silver-grey, with a broad black band. So attired, young Andalucía is 'on top of the world'.

To see the Andalucían at his most spectacular, you must attend the Easter *feria* at Sevilla, where handsome youths, with pretty girls behind them, ride up and down on slim, proud horses. The Andalucían riding costume surpasses anything I have ever seen for elegance: the short jacket of black, silver-grey, chestnut-red or plum, worn over a frilled cambric shirt, the coat itself frogged, and faced with velvet. The long, tight trousers are shaped like a corset to the wearer's waist, at once defining its slimness and dispensing with belt and braces, and carried high up the shoulder-blades in twin points. Add lacquered boots and a broad, flat-crowned hat of hatter's plush with a chinstrap, and you have the picture of the Sevillan buck, displaying his graces and those of his girl before an admiring audience.

The girls' dresses for the same occasion are of many-flounced muslin, spotted and bound in plain colour; if the small shawl is worn, it is knotted behind the wearer's waist. Headdresses vary from the high comb, with a rose or a carnation thrust behind the ear, to the riding hat which lends an air of charming coquetry to a pretty face. A few girls ride their own horses, and wear smartly cut habits that imitate the men's; side saddle is *de rigueur*, but the general standard of riding (apart from that of the *ganaderos*, who are to be distinguished by their fine, flaring chaps of russet leather) is low. The only people, apart from the military, who can now afford to ride are the *nouveaux riches*, whose traditions do not include the noble art of the saddle.

Such spectacles are, however, as much of an excrescence on modern Andalucía as the magnificent relics of its Moorish occupation. The shawl (except as worn by the gipsies) has vanished with the mantilla, and none but the foolhardy tourist falls to the lure of 'genuine antiques' in the shop windows. The shawls of today are either unscrupulous fakes or frankly modern Gilbraltese products; a real old shawl, fine enough to pass through a wedding ring, loaded with its delicate embroideries, with its heavily knotted fringe, comes on the market only when the poverty of its owner forces her to delve among the family heirlooms. Such a specimen is certainly worth its weight in gold.

Nor are any more of the old, shaped mantillas to be found, with their shoulder-flounces of fine lace; the modern mantilla, as worn by a few young and pretty women at the bullfight, is a long, straight piece of heavy black or white lace, and all depends on the art with which it is arranged. One sees it now and again worn by an over-enthusiastic foreigner—with deplorable results. The correct tenue of the mantilla is as formal as that of the hunting stock, and the assistance of a hotel chambermaid (who has probably never worn one in her life) is not to be relied upon for that complicated affair of combs, pins, folds, and the rightly or wrongly placed crescent of carnations.

The shawl, it may be added, is never worn for the *corrida*, but is draped over the front of the box, adding its beauty to the splendour of the spectacle.

The prettiest form of head covering is, to my mind, the *madrona*, worn by a few elderly women: a fan-shaped net of heavy black chenille, which is worn behind the comb, covering the heavy knot of raven-black hair, with its pointed edge, sometimes finished with little balls of chenille, spread out to cover the shoulders.

Thus, on occasion, does Andalucía conform to the tourist ideal, and fulfil the promise of the travel folders, flinging over the homespun texture of its workaday existence a mantle of illusion as fragile as its easy compliments. A short journey through Andalucía is apt to resolve itself into a perpetual banquet: so lavishly does the country fling its resources of natural beauty at the stranger's feet. To every hint of gaiety, of celebration, the Andalucían responds like a flower swinging towards the sun; his pride, no less than the natural urbanity of his character, obliges him to contribute in every possible fashion to the enjoyment and comfort of the foreigner.

Nowhere is this more strongly exemplified than in Sevilla, where hospitality was pressed upon us in a degree the more embarrassing in that we were allowed no opportunities to return it. Impossible to pay for a glass of wine, for a plate of *gambas*; cars placed at one's disposal, expeditions planned— the only thought in everyone's mind seemed to be that of showing off his city and its surroundings to their best advantage. A friendly and benign curiosity, not in the least offensive, surrounds one's most trivial actions, gives one a sense of affectionate supervision, all for one's own good, against which only a churl could rebel.

The murmured 'Go with God' sent after one at dusk by a peasant on a lonely road is the summary of Andalucía's attitude to humanity. When the feast is ended and the lamps expire, that 'Go with God' lingers like a benediction on one's day.

CHAPTER III

PANORAMA II

THE Andalucían is first an individual, then a contemplative. Action interests him less than motives—that is to say, the discussion of motives, their philosophic content, rather than any moral or practical issue that may be involved.

In taking stock of the Andalucían one must first take stock of his traditions: for he is overwhelmingly a traditionalist, and it is only by recognizing and respecting this fact that one can arrive at more than a superficial sympathy with his character.

The Moorish influence accounts for many of the traits which the would-be agitator find so disconcerting. The overwhelming lassitude, the disposition towards fatalism, defeat any efforts to make the Andalucían exert himself on his own behalf; as the cynicism and power of finding ridiculous that which other people find impressive makes him a bad recruit to causes of whose importance he is never convinced.

He is a dweller in the present—a present which is conditioned by the past; he tolerates innovations, so far as these benefit him personally—he is, for example, a devotee of the radio, which he employs at its loudest possible pitch, possibly as an extension of his own exuberant personality—but they must literally be delivered at his door and planted on his hearth before he will avail himself of them.

The future does not interest him—quite frankly, he does not believe in it. He is acutely conscious of being here only for his little day, and what comes after is the affair of his survivors. To those who attempt to rouse his resentment of systems of government or political measures he is courteously attentive, may even put up some histrionic response:

but sooner or later his fine, *rusée* smile will dispose alike of the subject and of its propounder. When have kings or governments ever moved at the bidding of the people? What comes of revolution except some trivial alterations benefiting a few interested parties? And, supposing some little measure is proposed, that might advantage him or his immediate circle—it will never be put into effect during his lifetime.

This, obviously, is an attitude excessively irritating to people of action, whose instinct on recognizing that a thing is wrong is to take measures to set it in order. To them, such an attitude of nonchalance derives from a culpable indolence, an irresponsible *laisser faire*. Yet those who have taken some pains to know him regard the Andalucían neither as indolent (although the climate lends itself to indolence) nor frivolous. His conduct, indeed, is mainly dictated by a kind of cheerful and intelligent pessimism, that is satisfied to make the best of the present without foolish adventurings into the future.

What are the things that matter to the Andalucían? In order of importance, they may be summarized as follows:

1. HIMSELF. His family. His means of livelihood. His amusements, of which the chief is conversation.
2. His own town. Its history. Its traditions. Its present-day government, and its rivalry with neighbouring townships.
3. His province. Its regional character and occupations.
4. Practical questions of politics and religion.
5. Spain, as a whole.
6. Europe and the rest of the civilized world.

Evidently this graduation of interests does not make either for personal prosperity or for the betterment of the race. It explains, in part, why Andalucía, a land running with milk and honey, indescribably rich in its vineyards, its olivares, its orange and lemon groves, its grazing grounds, is yet a land of the direst poverty; why there is no awakening the Andalucían, whether proprietor or serf, to the ideals of communal good. It is easy for the republican to blame the monarchy, the monarchist to blame the republic, the atheist to blame the Church, and the Church—very properly—to ignore its critics; the fault lies deeper—in the red earth, so impregnated with centuries of fatalism that latter-day enlightenment can shed no illumination into the sunken forests of the past.

While there is the sun on the wall, the Andalucían will prefer to bask in its rays, rather than enter into the heat and struggle of an effort towards betterment. It is an attitude not without wisdom: an attitude that would have been approved by the followers of Lâo Tsze—this contentment with the minimum, this rejection of all that the maximum brings of strife, heartburning, bitterness.

But there is another side to the picture. Any visitor to Andalucía must be struck by the numbers of young, and, on the whole, well-dressed young men who seem to have nothing to do between dawn and eve but sit in the cafés, eyeing the pretty girls, drinking, perhaps, a coffee, smoking a cigarette, extending their feet in lordly fashion to the shoeblacks who infest all the places of refreshment. Follow one of these young men throughout a day, and in all likelihood you will never see him eat. At dusk he sneaks to the *reja* of one of the large houses, through which his mother—the cook or the kitchenmaid—thrusts a plate of broken meats that he devours with the furtive hunger of a half-starved animal.

Offer him, in pity, a job of work, and he will smile vaguely and drift away. It is this poison of parasitism which is the ruin of the South. Rather than take up a paid task, involving regular hours and attention to duty, these city youths will go hungry, weak and penniless, sponging on their female relatives for their cheap smart clothes, their pocket-money and their packet of *canarios*. They suffer no loss of face, it is their privilege as males, boldly claimed and, by the women, humbly accepted, to live dependent on feminine self-sacrifice and industry.

The working women of Andalucía are its mute, inglorious heroines; it is they who, for the most part, carry the burden of the household, are mainly responsible for its upkeep, work themselves to the bone for the all-conquering male who, when the first transports of courtship and early marriage have worn off, regards them as practically as he regards his ass, and with considerably less sentiment than he regards his dog.

Year by year these women go mechanically through the processes of childbirth; the children die—of fevers or infantile maladies, or syphilis, or starvation—and there is no time to mourn one before another is on the way. The more sensible visit the clinics, have their injections—and get infected again. A blind baby is born: one more dependent on the many organizations for the care of the blind that are to be found in every town. When it grows up it will learn the guitar, will be led about and earn its dubious keep from the facile compassion of those who continue to propagate its fellows.

But at the outbreak of the civil war, a new race of women was growing up in Andalucía. In the larger towns, serious groups of young students, with bare heads and socks instead of stockings wrinkled round their bare brown ankles, flocked towards the universities with bundles of text-books under their arms.

They were not having an easy time, those sober young rebels, belonging, many of them, to harem-like homes, where a nineteenth-century routine continued to be observed by their elderly female relatives. It was not surprising that their increasingly enfranchized minds reached out beyond the boundaries of Andalucía: that the ambition of each was to gain her livelihood elsewhere, anywhere outside that radius of intellectual suffocation, of tradition and superstition; and it was sad to think of that hardly-won knowledge being dissipated outside of the region it might have served so well.

On the severe young faces was written the determination not to grow up like their mothers and grandmothers, into fat, chocolate-eating granadinas, or sevillanas, or cordo-bésas: with no conversation but scandal and no interests save family politics, no activities save in spying on each other's actions, and no relation save the sexual one with the men they married.

Their scorn for tradition reached out and embraced religion and regional custom; no more combs and mantillas on Sundays of festival, no dressing up the *patio* for Santa

Cruz, no amorous whispering at the *rejas* . . . however one might applaud the march of progress, it was difficult to withhold a feeling of regret from these young creatures who, in denying their soil, were dedicated to sadness.

In other parts of Spain they seemed to belong, to be a natural expression of advancing civilization; in Andalucía they were aloof as expatriates, existing by force of their internal loyalties in a twilight, if not of active disapproval, at least of misunderstanding.

For the average Andaluza, when one has exhausted her superficial attractions, her bright, conscious glitter and volatility of temperament, is a poor companion. She has the faults of her virtues: an overweening vanity, an excessive jealousy towards her own sex. After her marriage she ceases to exist as an individual. Nothing in her education or her upbringing compensates for the rapid fading of her physical charms; fretful, malicious, neurotic, her life narrows itself to the company of her children, of her husband's female relatives who, under pretext of safeguarding the honour of the house, watch her like lynxes through the earlier years of matrimony, and, as time goes on, gradually absorb her into their feminine cabala of petty intrigue.

Once a week, on Sunday, she may accompany her husband (of whom otherwise she sees little) to the café, or to a picture theatre; a family reunion may make a little break in the monotony of her week. Otherwise she has little to do save sit behind the *rejas*, watching the passers-by, and go to mass.

She stitches, she reads—the lightest of novels—she waters the plants on her balcony, she feeds her birds. But above all she talks—oh, that endless web of trivial and often poisonous nothings, that entangles not only the family itself, but the domestics and the dressmaker and the manicurist who come once a week to attend to the ladies' hands! It is not to be wondered at that the average Englishwoman makes few real friendships among the Andalucían women; or that, in search of realities, I found myself turning to the working-class wives and daughters, who, if they have a little less education, have all the fibre, the human and respectable qualities that contact with reality entails.

The men, on the contrary, are truly companionable. Genial, generous, and excellent conversationalists, their habit of regarding every question from a detached and impersonal angle is as cooling as fine rain. They love the abstract; their cynicism cauterizes sentimentality. Religion and politics they are apt to treat as extravagances for children —which does not prevent their going regularly to confession, or gathering in full force for a political meeting. From the outpourings of a sensationalist, such as La Pasionaria, they derive exactly the same pleasure as they receive from a performance in the theatre; the following week they will listen with equal attention and artistic detachment to an orator from the opposite camp.

The most inapposite criticism of the Andalucían that I ever heard (from an Englishwoman) was that he is childish. I find him, on the contrary, almost horrifyingly adult, in his ripe and reasoned attitude to topics on which most speakers have a rather tiresome way of becoming hysterical. It is as though all that he is, he is with deliberation: having considered other possibilities, and dismissed them as unworthy of a person of experience and philosophy. The foreigner who persists in regarding the Andalucían as the elegant buffoon which he often chooses to play is himself a victim of the Andalucían sense of humour, which delights in such little misunderstandings. His essential evasiveness, as well as his desire to please, incline him always to express the opinion which he thinks will be most acceptable to his listener; it is therefore less upon what one hears, than upon what one observes that the stranger must take his stand in attempting to form conclusions.

In contrast with his women-folk, the Andalucían has a very active and vivid life of the mind, as apart from the life of the body—which latter he treats with a frank realism that neither excuses nor conceals matters that no true Southerner regards as culpable. My own impression is that the Andaluz pours much more of his passion into his music, his poetry and his bullfighting than into the (for him) purely utilitarian act of making love.

Among certain young Andalucíans a cult for heartiness

is gaining some ground; 'el futbol' has many devotees who, after a period in which the game itself was somewhat less important than leaning up against the post office in one's shorts and blazer, to capture the eyes of the enraptured feminine, have settled down seriously to play the game.

Here, then, is a little of what underlies the 'romanticism' which foreigners insist upon finding in Andalucía. Apart from its colouring and its days of *fiesta*, it is hard to imagine a country less romantic, more uncompromisingly realistic in its attitude to life. You will come across the professional romantic in the taverns and on the outskirts of the bullring; you will find him shining shoes, or scribbling bad verse for the price of a glass of manzanilla; but you will never find him in a position of responsibility or of material well-being.

The Andaluz is an excellent commercial; he will sell you his town, his belongings and his personality with a charming grace, and—let there be no misunderstanding—not always for money. Money, in fact, is a commodity which needs delicate handling, at least by the foreigner, in Andalucía. Goodwill is of more value than cash; the Andalucían is passionately anxious to capture your goodwill, and, it goes without saying, your admiration.

If he has lost some of that splendid, lofty indifference to money which was his under the monarchy, is he to be blamed for it? Times are changed; wine no longer flows like water—or rather, the rich source of the flow is no longer there. Time was, the *commerciante* in wines waxed fat on his commissions on the noblest vintages; now he economizes, and prays heaven to send him an agency in *Anis del Mono*, for the impoverished upper classes can no longer afford the great wines, and the new rich have yet to cultivate their palates.

And in spite of the commercial instinct, one thing is bound to strike the traveller: that publicity—advertisement —is in its infancy. The Andalucían with something to sell— be it men's suitings or seats for the bullfight—would rather trust to the mouth-to-mouth recommendation that served his grandparents than risk his capital on the indeterminate services of a publicity manager. Now and again, if there is a

37

sale or some special event of public interest, a few little handbills may be circulated, but a Granada outfitter who had some overcoats to sell was regarded as a dangerous innovationist because he sent out a sandwich-man on stilts, who tottered and rustled among the branches before the café de la Alameda, not only to the peril of his own limbs, but to the nervous prostration of the spectators. You may walk your feet sore in search of an advertisement for the imminent bullfight—of which your waiter at the café will give you all necessary information.

What then, one may be asked, when one has exhausted the charms of the tourist Andalucía and come down to the bedrock which is indicated in this chapter—what then constitutes the pleasure of living in such a country, of which the general impression is one of enervation and backwardness? Yet how false such an impression must be!

Fundamentally, one gains a fresh perspective on life. The fret and fever of our civilization, the mania of energy for energy's sake, and not for the result achieved, gradually fade out of one's system. Contemplation, an art almost lost to the Western world, becomes second nature—'nothing is either good or bad but thinking makes it so' no longer a timeworn *cliché* but a governing factor in existence.

Shreds of forgotten philosophies drift back into one's mind like the shreds of mist that drift down the mountains: the mountains which, wherever one goes, whether in town or country, seem always in one's consciousness.

'The still mind of the sage is the mirror of heaven and earth, the glass of all things. Vacancy, stillness, placidity, tastelessness, quietude, silence and non-action; this is the level of heaven and earth, and the perfection of the Tao.' Thus Kwang-Tze. And Epictetus, amidst the disturbance of times not unlike our own:

'If thou wouldst advance, be content to let people think thee senseless and foolish as regards external things. Wish not ever to seem wise, and if ever thou shalt find thyself accounted to be somebody, then mistrust thyself.'

And, at the height of one's utmost mistrust and weakness, these soaring words for one's comfort·

' "What, then, if one come and find me alone and slay me?" Fool!—not thee, but thy wretched body. Thou art a little soul bearing up a corpse.'

It is thoughts such as these—salutary and soothing thoughts—that take charge of one's spirit through the long, timeless Andalucían days: compelling the surrender of one's restless will to a wisdom born, not of the minds of man, but of the rhythms of nature. Vacancy, stillness, placidity, tastelessness, quietude, silence and non-action: these are the gifts of the Andalucían gods, which, as one much harassed with life's fitful fevers, I took thankfully, and which to this day I lay as balm to my spirit.

CHAPTER IV

GRANADA

ALGECIRAS, Cadiz, Jérez de la Frontera, Sevilla, Ronda, Cordoba leave their coloured shadows upon my memories of that first mute journey, of which a record in my diary recalls the curious sense of isolation:

'. . . listening to the powerful gutterals, the resonant vowels of southern Spanish speech gives one a feeling of convalescence after a serious illness: one is so limp, so quiescent, so out of it all! A bit of seaweed, mindless, emotionless, rocking on an Iberian tide; an idiot, wandering inoffensively among people whose protective instinct is roused by her untroublesome behaviour. With what patience they watch over one, bearing with one's impenetrable stupidity, saving one from the results of one's indiscretions, encouraging one with little gestures of benevolence and goodwill.

'One's senses sharpen from day to day; words still mean nothing, but colours, shapes, sounds take on new significance. I really begin to think that *talking* is the least satisfactory form of communication between human beings; its possibilities of misinterpretation are almost hair-raising when one comes to think about it; whereas a look, a sign are unmistakable. I am losing my pity for the dumb . . .'

Later on, when I revisited most of these towns, it was surprising to discover how bright and accurate were some of those unprompted impressions, for which I was dependent wholly on my eyes, and on a vague quantity known as 'instinct'. During that first journey when, as I carefully avoided the tourist caravanserai, I probably did not open my lips a dozen times between Algeciras and Sevilla, or half a dozen times between Sevilla and Cordoba, I was registering vividly a new and entrancing scene. In Sevilla, where English, or French, are generally understood, if not spoken, I found myself disconcerted by having to talk; my own language creaked on my tongue and in my ears, and I was conscious of an overwhelming urge to again escape into silence.

The glittering day-time whiteness of Cadiz, its pearly evening beauty were to come back to me later in the words of a song; and if I could not subscribe to the description of its people 'living like butterflies'—*viven como las mariposas*—Cadiz having impressed me as a singularly active and business-like little town, I joined warmly in the triumphant conclusion: '*Mir' Usted la gracia que tienen en Ca'i'* ! "

Small wonder if the language defeats the stranger—that richly slurred Andaluz, so different from what is printed in one's little phrase book (mine lost, of course, before the Algeciras dust had vanished from my shoe-tops), which drops its final and sometimes even its middle consonants, which changes B's into V's and V's into B's, and casually slips an R in the place of an L! When '*olvide*' becomes '*orbide*,' what is the poor foreigner to do about it? In some parts of Andalucía, if one speaks the *castellano*, the natives do not understand. They are very proud of their Andaluz which, even in Madrid, is accorded the dignity of a separate language. Some of the newspapers print their bullfighting news in Andaluz; it has its own poetry, its own literature—and a friend of mine writes to me always in Andaluz which, although I was 'reared' on it, and hardly heard the *castellano* until I visited the north, is curiously defeating to the eye.

The sparkle of Cadiz, the austere and reserved dignity of Jeréz de la Frontera, the remoteness of Ronda, the golden grace of Cordoba, the narrow streets, like cañons, of Jaén, not to mention a score of little towns like Medinacelli, Archidona, Antequera, Almuñecar, whose lovely names 'go chiming through my head', gradually united to make a picture of the living beauty which is Andalucía.

One learns to dawdle through a day, to stop half a dozen times in the course of a morning stroll to drink small glasses of the sharp, dry manzanilla, and to eat shrimps at the little tables on the plazas: to have one's shoes cleaned almost as often (so much the better if your shoeblack is a hunchback; he will take it as a compliment if you touch his crooked shoulder to bring yourself luck); to buy lottery tickets— largely because the vendor is so meek, so anxious not to interrupt your conversation or your pleasure; to crunch sugared almonds, to accept snowballs of perfumed jasmine, made by pulling the flower-heads off their stalks and mounting them on split straws. Life drops into slow motion. You are between a dream and a dream.

One does a little sight seeing. (I am assuming, of course, that one is not attached to a tourist party.) The lonely traveller is sometimes, I find, beset with a foolish, intellectual snobbery that rejects local 'lions' simply because they are lions. The difference between travelling alone and travelling in company is that one sees what one wishes to see, without effort, without obligation—above all, without the detestable sense of duty which takes the gilt off the best gingerbread. It is sheer folly, in visiting Sevilla, not to see the museum of Cristóbal Colon, the old cockpit, the bullring which is the queen of all bullrings, with its bright white walls, and its perforated battlements of yellow ochre; the House of Pilatus, the Giralda tower round which the little brown and white hawks fly all day long; not to stroll in the Alcazar gardens, not to attend a mass at the cathedral. These are affairs, not of tourism, but of common intelligence.

Who visits Jeréz and omits the bodegas has not visited Jeréz, and no amount of prejudice against Moorish architecture—of which, let's admit it, I for one can quickly have enough—can excuse the omission of the mosque in a visit to Cordoba.

In almost every Andalucían town there is one church that is worth seeing, and a dozen which are not. The main thing is to take all this casually in one's stride; not to make a business of it; not, above all, to worry over details that have escaped one's notice, or to burden one's conscience with historical data or guide-book references. If, later, enthusiasm inclines one to intensive study, so much the better; but on a first visit it is the general impression which matters, which builds up one's concept of the town or province as a whole, and increases one's love and knowledge in some subtle fashion that organized sightseeing tends to repress.

It was at Cordoba that I began to understand a little Spanish. I could, at any rate, make a good guess at what people were talking about; I had learned, through repetition, two or three trite little sentences for personal currency. At the same time I began to lose that feeling of phantom-like separation from a world of actualities; I recognized, not without regret, that my period of happy irresponsibility was drawing to a close.

We came to Granada a little after midnight, on a night of stars and full moon. There was the drive through the lower town, brightly lit and commonplace; then the mountainous ascent beneath the elms of the Alhambra, which ended in a broken path and a tiny house blasted with moonlight, against which the notes of the nightingales fell like drops of liquid silver. Half an hour later I was standing on my balcony, overlooking such a scene as I had never felt could have existence outside the pages of a romance.

The little Carmen totters on the edge of a terraced precipice that ends on the level of the plain. A smother of wistaria, of palms, pomegranates, cypress and centuries-old myrtle clothes the lower terraces, below which—far below—like a handful of topaz tossed on a sapphire-blue cloth, the lights of Granada burned, golden, steady, sometimes in isolated grandeur, sometimes in a cluster illuminating some façade or fragment of architecture above whose summits blazed the great white stars. Beyond, like a dreaming sea, shoaled with imperceptible gradations of blue and emerald, the plain rolled to the foot of the farther mountains, which, curving southward, soared into the Sierra Nevada, whose eternally snow-laden peaks shone white in the light of the moon. Save for the chirr of the cicadas, the fitful bursts of song from the nightingales, the gurgles of a hidden stream, there was not a sound.

Closing my shutters, turning towards my stark little room, with the palsied pink walls, the primitive oddments of furniture, the one staring electric light bulb swarmed around with moths, I knew I had reached my journey's end. There were Jaén, Almería, Malaga still to be visited; I rejected them all. For the first time since setting out on my travels, I unpacked all my baggage, and metaphorically took possession of that patch of Andalucían earth which, for the better part of three years, was to be my happy home.

The town of Granada, it may be said, for the benefit of those who are topographically inclined, is of all Andalucían cities the most isolated; it is a dead end, it leads nowhere, and one does not pass it on the way to anywhere else. To reach it from north, south, east or west—unless one is travelling by road—one has to diverge miles, by way of a melancholy little junction called Bobadilla, from which one backs one's tracks along the branch line which alone serves Granada.

Backed by its mountain ranges, it has preserved through centuries its dignity of isolation, its indifference to all that happens outside its walls, as today it preserves its fine contempt of its *arriviste* neighbour Malaga—'neighbour' in the sense that it is not more than a three-and-a-half hour drive through the *sierras* from the Granada Alameda to tne Malaga one.

It has paid the price of its aristocracy in the gradual seeping away of trade from its portals; Granada has no industries —if one excepts the little Albaicin factory where weaving goes on as it has gone on for a dozen generations; where the Alpujárran tapestries grow daily upon the looms, and the bundles of dyed yarn in every shade of crimson and purple, blue, green, orange and tender fawn swing from the balconies. Some pottery is made—coarse blue-and-green stuff, painted on a grey-blue glaze over red clay. There are some outlying vineyards and plantations of sugar cane. In the summer, Granada exists on her tourist population; in the winter, she . . . exists.

Yet, to visualize Granada as a town infested during the pleasantest months by tourists is to gain a wrong impression. They come, they go—mysteriously: leaving no mark whatever on the life of the town. You may find them, clotted in

44

the Alhambra, the Generalife, the Cartuja or the Cathedral, but their stay is, usually, of the briefest. One would say they are frightened away by the cold, unblinking reserve of the place, of its inhabitants, who have a way of behaving as if they were not there; when the sights have been seen, there is nothing for them to do, and nowhere for them to be.

The cafés serve them politely, but show no enthusiasm for their presence. Few venture into the taverns—which are the heart of Granada—for the average foreigner is not accustomed to tavern society; he is embarrassed, made shy by it. So, after a little uneasy wandering, they are glad, on the whole, to climb into their autobuses, their hired limousines, and whirl away to Malaga—as glad as they are to be able to say that they have seen the Alhambra, and taken snapshots of Aunt Emma and the twins in the Court of the Lions. Granada is 'too Spanish' for them, too indifferent to their foreign prejudices, their odd tastes, their bacon-and-eggs breakfasts, their sacred afternoon tea!

The town of Granada divides itself naturally into three parts, of which the modern district, with the shopping centre and the flats of the more prosperous bourgeoisie, forms the lowest level. Even this so-called 'modern' Granada is honeycombed through with relics of the past; there is the network of narrow streets surrounding the Zácatin—the old 'Sierpes' of Granada, where there is only foot traffic; there is the Cathedral property, there is that sinister, broken-down region between the Reyes Católicos (now Granada's principal street) and the Alameda, which always seems to me the dead heart of Granada, with its high, Moorish buildings—most of them brothels.

On the two hills that enclose this space triangularly, and are separated by the River Darro, are placed respectively the Alhambra and the Generalife, with their surrounding villas and the Albaicin, the old Moorish quarter, which, with the Sacromonte, houses the gipsies and their caves. This part of the town is not favoured by the tourist, partly on account of its malodorous heat—the very stones frizzle at noon on a June day—and partly for the gipsy children who pester one for alms; but it is indisputably the most picturesque and characteristic quarter, apart from the Alhambra itself.

Here the precipitous little streets, often narrow enough to be spanned by the extension of one's arms, climb up-wards towards the tower of San Bartolomé—once a muezzin tower, now a-flutter with the household washing and bright with the pot-plants of its secular occupants; and here live the people who, by reason of the hardships of their lot, have dragged themselves out of the dream that smothers Granada and face hour by hour a world of grim reality which their more prosperous neighbours ignore.

I have no recollection of my first visit to the tavern of Doña Luisa, right in the shadow of San Bartolomé, or of how I became involved with the little Albaicin colony whose affairs brought a lively interest into my life which would have been lacking, had I surrendered to the mandragora of my Alhambra existence.

The patio, with its ridges of turquoise blue tiles, its Moor-ish basin, with a thread of fountain and sleepy goldfish, its canopy of vines and its rocking-chairs under the quinces, is a minuscule paradise in the heart of a slum. Everything is very clean; you could 'eat off the floor'; the wine is like ice, the olives large, fat, juicy. If you stay out of doors, you are not pestered by the flies, which are the horror of the Albai-cin; no amount of individual cleanliness will keep them out of a house—those metallic leviathans that gorge themselves on the offal of the alleys. The *patio* is the rendezvous of all the flamenco singers, the granadinos who seek a quiet, friendly evening above the simmering heat of the town: as well as of everyone who has a new piece of gossip, a morsel of scandal, a grievance or a triumph to ventilate. In short, the whole life of Granada passes in panorama through Luisa's *patio* between dawn and dusk.

Sometimes, after a longer session than usual of music and dancing, I have spent the night up there: in a room whiter than moonlight, with a little unglazed *reja* that opened on the side street, through which, at the earliest streak of dawn, came the fanfaronade of the Albaicin cocks, the harsh '*Arré!*' of the donkey-driver, mingling with the clop-clop of tiny hooves, the swish of the brushwood burdens against the walls, the bleating of goats. One rose at five, to wash in the ice-cold water of the well; at six one sat under the quinces to eat *bollos* and drink the steaming bowls of coffee. Unfortunately, my Alhambra household did not approve of such outings, and the more-in-sorrow-than-in-anger expressions that greeted me on my return were enough to cast a blight over the rest of the day. If I ever had a headache or an attack of fever, it was '*la mala gente*' who had given them to me.

Luisa and her husband, Miguel, were the first to make me free of this new world, on whose brink I faltered, hesitant as one must be who knows nothing, not even the language, and is fearful by some false step of prejudicing the rest. They had the natural breeding of the Andalucían peasant—although I have often suspected a streak of gipsy in Luisa's veins. For all her ignorance, her superstition, prejudice and vanity, she was the only woman I met for a long time who inspired me to something closer than mere acquaintanceship. It was an amusing relationship, all tangled up with our cynical appreciation of each other's shortcomings, my openly expressed disapproval of many of her actions and our absolutely parallel sense of what was ridiculous, which we discovered long before we could communicate other than by signs and grimaces.

From her sparkling gaiety, from Miguel's intelligent goodwill, I gathered boldness; soon I was throwing out tendrils right and left. If I made a mistake, Luisa would set it right; if I were uncertain, Miguel would resolve my doubts. And I started to speak Spanish—of a sort—with a suddenness that was like turning on a tap. I was so impatient to understand the conversations that went on around me—the bullfighters, the hard-faced, handsome countrymen, the guitarristas, the gipsies, the priests who gathered at the Villa Luisa—that I went boldly into taverns, I listened to what was said in cafés, by the servants in the kitchen, by customers in the shops, by the women in the hairdressing parlours . . . and one day I went to the church of Nuestra Señora de las Augustias, so high, so splendid in the golden replica of the crown the last Alfonso gave her.

She is known throughout the country as the Miraculous virgin, and the great fans of candles spread at her feet never sink in their sockets, because before one candle has burned an inch or two down, it is removed and replaced by another —so importunate are the Granadinos in their calls upon her mercy.

I bought a long candle and watched it lit, and, while the flame blended into the golden penumbra of the rest, I asked her to let me write one good book.

CHAPTER V

ALHAMBRA

Oᴏ the Alhambra itself everything has been written; those *patios* echoing with the silver sounds of fountains, the sweet-scented, forbidden gardens upon which one looks through tall *rejas* set in embrasures that invite repose, that iridescence of *azulejo* and dizzying honeycomb of vaulting must be part of the imagination of every person who has ever read a book about Spain.

Is it matter for wonder if some of those who visit them today meet a small, cold shock of disappointment in the reality? — if, enervated by the chanting of guides, the charibaria of foreign voices, the clicking of cameras, they take away the impression of an empty magnificence, of ground from which almost all of its original significance has been trampled by the feet of tourists?

A pre-eminent reason for living in Granada is, to my mind, to be able to visit the Alhambra at any hour: to choose one's time and one's mood, one's company or one's solitude for entering those strange, entrancing and disturbing courts; above all, to see it when no guides are there, to shatter the contemplative mood with their trite little discourses. To see the Alhambra when it is cool with sunrise, or flaming with sunset, or dreadfully black and white under the moon is the only way to know it. It calls for not a little patience and diplomacy; it is not a privilege to be bought as one buys seats for the bullfight.

A single daylight visit can give one but the shell of the mystery, the skeleton of an historical miracle which, whether or not one happens to like Moorish architecture, must leave a deep impression of awe and reverence within the soul. But really to feel the Alhambra, to experience something of its past, and to animate the dry bones of its guide-book history, there is no time like the sunset hour: when the warm stones give up their ancient emanations as the myrtles give up their perfume, when the shadows are long, when no colour is quite positive and no shape quite distinct, and the thud of a falling orange sets up a disproportionate reverberation in the darkling patio and in one's own heart; when the bats have started their swift nocturnal dance, the goldfish lie like motionless flakes of bright metal in their long pools, and the snow-white pigeons slumber on the sloping eaves like rejected shuttlecocks.

Now and again, on summer nights, in the great adjoining unfinished palace of Carlos Quinto, there is a *concurso* of *flamenco*, when the instrumentalists scatter their bravura of guitar and bandurría, and the voices of the singers, ringing against the stars, fall like the splinters of the past into those silent, listening courts; when past and present fuse, when *el ultimo sospiro del Moro* breathes in every long-drawn phrase supported by a modern cantador, whose inspiration, whether or not he is aware of it, derives from that age of Moorish supremacy; whose very notes are those which, before the coming of the Catholic kings, drew to the pierced lattices that soft, gazelle-eyed multitude, whose graces survive in their decendants to this day.

Of the Alhambra phantoms—of the Abencerrage knights who retread their doom in the *patio* at certain glimpses of the moon, of the ghostly dogs that haunt the Torres Vermejas— I have nothing to say; Washington Irving, whose false claim to have had lodgings in the Alhambra itself is vaunted by his countrymen and was indignantly denied by Doña Laura, as well as by the oldest of the guides, whose father could remember the temerarious American, has written a book of dubious history and more dubious legend in which he refers to some of the occult happenings inside the walls. Of these all that I know is hearsay. My Rosario would never pass by the Vermilion Towers after dusk, and one of the night-watchmen told me of the tread of a mailed foot that had disturbed him repeatedly during his night rounds. In the two villas I occupied in the Alhambra precincts I had experience of the unquiet spirits who are said to haunt the place.

I am a little shy of telling 'ghost stories', especially when they hinge upon personal experience, but as these in some degree coloured my sojourn in the Alhambra and infected my attitude to my surroundings, they may as well stand, as briefly as possible, here.

The first was on the night of my arrival; when a repeated knock sounded on one of the two doors of my bedroom, disturbing me not at all, since I took it for granted it might be a servant bringing hot water, or, seeing the light under the door, knocking to see if it was occupied. But when I had opened the door several times to find no one, it struck me as a little odd; and the last time I opened, and looked across the empty, moonlit apartment next door, the sound of old, tired footsteps, in loose slippers, dragging away in the distance, roused my curiosity and tempted me to follow. Crossing the empty room quickly, I came out on the square entrance hall, with its stairway leading down to the lower floor.

I had not been downstairs, but so strong was my curiosity that I hurried down, in the wake of the weary footsteps, to find nothing, no one in the lower rooms. I cannot remember at this distance of time whether or not I was frightened. I think I cannot have been very frightened, for I went back to bed, and to sleep, with nothing but a vague sense of eeriness, which I put down to my strange surroundings, to disturb my rest.

Later on, when I got to know Doña Laura, I described the incident to her. I can see her now, peering up at me with those bright brown eyes: deciding whether I was one of those fool English who would get her house a bad name. Eventually, in that booming voice that should have belonged to a giantess rather than to a little old woman on whose head it would have been convenient to rest my elbow, she said, grudgingly: 'This room was one of the dungeons in which they—*los Reyes Catolicos*—incarcerated the captured Moors. They say there is one who walks . . . I know nothing about it. But people say they have heard it when they sleep in the house for the first time.'

Evidently the wanderer's curiosity was satisfied, for I never again heard anything during my sojourn in the House of the Dead Moor. But that second experience, which took place when I was sleeping all alone in the little villa that faced it, was another matter.

None of my friends had wanted me to stay there alone. I had pooh-poohed their solicitude, rejoicing in that moment when the servants went home, and I had the place to myself. With the great *cancela* locking me in as securely as if I were in a prison, and *rejas* at all of the ground-floor windows, what had I to fear? Interpreting the anxiety of my friends as some granadino convention, something like not bowing first to male acquaintances in the street, and not sharing a box at the theatre excepting with a female companion, I went to much pains to explain that, although I was ready in all ways to accept the formalities of the country, I must be allowed at night to enjoy my accustomed solitude during which, as in England, I did most of my work.

I had gone to bed, in my doorless little room, with the thin curtains swinging gently in the night breeze that blew straight through the open window of the *sala* and the tiny window in a corner of the bedroom which looked out on the public footpath, when I heard the unmistakable sound of a foot stumbling on the stairs. My heart stopped beating. It was incredible—yet obvious—that someone had got into the house.

There was no telephone; nothing I could do but shriek— in the very doubtful hope that I might be heard from the Matamoros, whose occupants were by now, without question, sound asleep. I could not escape into the garden without passing the unknown maurauder, whose stealthy approach continued. I could hear the cautious turning at the top of the stairs, the tentative slide of a foot along the polished boards of the landing. The shriek—if I had decided on it—would not have come, for my throat was constricted as with a band of iron, and sweat was pouring down my face; I did the only thing I could—lay utterly still, with my eyes fixed upon the pale door curtain swaying in the moonlight.

The next thing that happened I would have questioned, doubting my powers of accuracy in the state of terror into which I had fallen, if the morning had not brought convincing proof of it. The curtain rang back along its brass rod; it must have done so, for there it was, drawn fully back in the morning, and the steps, now assured and leisurely, entered the room. I saw nothing, and remember nothing else, until I found Rosario sobbing over me in the morning.

'*Senora! Señora—madre mia de mi alma*, what has happened to the señora in the night?' The reason of her horror was explained when she helped me up and led me to the looking-glass.

I have no explanation to offer of this uncomfortable incident, which I think would not have disturbed me so much if it had happened in more familiar surroundings and away from those strange precincts. Alhambra stones are unquiet stones; no Granadino will deny it.

How should it be otherwise? The record of the Alhambra is a record of outrage and crime, of the indulgence of violent lusts, of the avenging of violent injuries, and there can be no peace in the soil which has entombed through many centuries its grim secrets.

What a *chronique scandaleuse* it could furnish—this little clutch of villas which makes up the Alhambra precincts! A record of petty but none the less poignant dramas, played out behind the *rejas* and the closely guarded cancelas of the mouldering houses which, withdrawn from vulgar publicity behind their tangle of trees, today yield up only the groups of servants who gossip at the gates, their brightly watchful eyes upon the passers-by. Their ears are goblets for every drop of gossip which falls like dew upon the drought of their empty days, and this most precious ichor is carried indoors, to nourish and revive the fading life within the crumbling walls.

Just occasionally, about the hour of sunset, one may catch a glimpse of this cherished life, shrouded and supported upon a domestic's arm, or propped on the threshold: an old, waxen head, draped in black, a face seamed with bitterness and eyes as dull as the coins which will presently be laid upon them. One more old Alhambra lady, putting on time until the Great Occasion—the greatest, since her marriage, in all her career.

And, struggle as one may against the morbid reflection, it cannot be thrust aside: that these Alhambra misses, who flirt their earrings and compress their hips into tight little flowered gowns and make girlish jokes among themselves, or flicker coy lashes at all the presentable granadino gentlemen, are on their way to becoming old Alhambra ladies. One's heart cries out to them to save themselves before it is too late: to tear themselves from the jealous and dangerous soil, from walls the colour of pale blood and from tree-roots that suck out like vampires the vitality of human beings.

Over how many shattered romances has the Alhambra brooded, since the curse of the Moor was laid upon it? And, looking back, who can avoid the corollary that never blooms the rose so red as upon soil fertilized by human suffering?

Clinging like martlets' nests to the crumbling rock, overlooking with the contemptuous aristocracy of age and tradition the new bungalows from which the radio shrieks unceasingly are two tiny villas: one so minute that it hardly distinguishes itself from the herbage which entangles it, the other stark in its decrepitude, taking the blaze of the sun, the beat of the hail upon a façade that has ceased to be of any colour whatever, upon *persanas* that flap their reedy rags across perilous balconies.

One has its little garden, its paradise of roses, its cypresses and morning glory, its tiny labyrinth of well-kept paths between low box edges, and its wistaria-shadowed loggia; the other has a tangle of myrtles and some dying palms, a mirador whose tumbledown ladder invites one to break one's neck for the sake of the view above, and a hen-run in which a few scraggy fowls philosophically await the knife, too wise and too languid to scratch in the sterile dust. The hens have much in common with the old Alhambra ladies: they, too, await their Great Occasion.

In each of these villas lives an old lady: foreigners both, but decades of domicile have conferred on each the gracious

54

title bestowed by Spaniards upon the elderly and distinguished of their sex. One is Doña Laura, the other Doña Mercédes. For each her house is a little tomb, in which the sinking flame of life is kept alight only by hatred and rivalry: for Doña Laura is ninety-seven and Doña Mercédes ninety-nine. Each speaks of the other with pitying contempt as 'that poor old woman'; at dusk they take it in turns each to pay the other a visit of curiosity and suspicion.

Leaning upon the arm of a servant who loathes her and wishes her dead, Doña Laura hobbles across to visit Doña Mercédes who, supported by her own domestic, watches with bright black eyes of malice the palsied advance of her rival. At a mere ninety-seven to be as decrepit as that!

'But of course,' Doña Mercédes explains, in her harsh, Americanized Spanish, to the servant, 'it is the drink that causes it.'

'*Ay-di-mi! Pobre di ella.*' A compassionate shrug conveys the other's pity for poor Doña Laura who, it is well known, is too poor to buy all the drink she would like.

At ninety-nine Doña Mercédes still takes her *paseo* unattended beneath the elms of the Generalife hill. A tottering column of dust-coloured silk, her sunshade, supported in a small, gloved hand, protects her beautiful little death's-head, with its rich covering of still luxuriant, dark grey hair. Current opinion is unanimous that, 'in her day' Doña Mercédes must have been very beautiful. She still has elegance, but talking to her is like talking across a wide stream, with the wind blowing back in the speaker's direction. The cracked instrument of her voice grates loudly upon one's ears, but of one's own remarks it is evident that Doña Mercédes receives a mere scattered echo. Out of their enormous black caverns, her eyes regard one with a resentful curiosity. One can hear—if the wind is in that direction—her rasped tongue tearing reputations to shreds, as she sits on her balcony with Doña Laura, whose deeper, booming tones are less distinct although no less reverberant.

Hating each other, they are forced to seek each other's society, for none other offers save those kindly calls of the vice-consul's unmarried sisters, which both the old ladies ungratefully resent yet grumble when they are not paid.

The relatively juvenile Doña Laura (for, after ninety, each year is as good as ten) makes up in intellectual for what she lacks in physical vigour. From the handsome old head, sunk between its arthritic shoulders, blaze out bright brown eyes which must once have been lovely, and can still light with an enchantingly sweet expression when she is pleased, or touched, or grateful about something. Doña Mercédes has outlived these tender reactions; her very thoughts clink like dried bones, and her one form of mental titillation is scandal: while Doña Laura still reads the classics—largely to nurture her scorn for Doña Mercédes.

The conversations of the two old ladies start always in the same way—with patronizing inquiries after each other's health, regarding which each enters into the frankest detail. Each is inclined to pooh-pooh the other's ailments: 'Of course, my dear, if you do not attend to yourself properly . . . I know, in *my* case . . .'

The angry duo of doctors' opinions opens, rises and swells, until both are shrieking in unison; socially taboo functions of the body are yelled to the welkin, their eccentricities named and strewn like dust upon the morning glory, that raises its cerulean cups to receive the nauseous dose. The two old rivals range savagely through the medical encyclopaedia, indifferent to the embarrassment of their neighbours who, in the next-door gardens, fidget and blush or giggle according to their generation and fashion of upbringing.

Having exhausted the possibilities of disease, they rush panting into the second phase of the dialogue, which is usually concerned with Doña Laura's paying guests—their appearance, their behaviour, their possible relationship with the aristocracy, and—sooner or later—their 'goings-on' in Granada.

'That writing woman had a man in her room last night!' comes in Doña Mercédes' parrot shriek, 'I saw their shadows on the balcony and sent Pepa to find out.'

Doña Laura booms that at least the writing woman pays her rent.

'Then perhaps', screams Doña Mercédes, 'you can pay me the hundred pesetas you borrowed from me last week?'

However the conversation starts, it ends always in the same manner: febrile rage crackling suddenly into fury. It is the noise of a dog-fight—the baying of Doña Laura dominating the yapping of an hysterical fox-terrier that precedes the collapse of Doña Mercédes.

We say next door: 'For God's sake, go and separate them!'

Pepa, her superb, oval face of a gipsy black with malice, folds her arms, nods viciously and grins.

'Let them go on until they drive each other mad—until they are taken to the asylum where they ought to be—until they drop dead at each other's feet!' is her complacent rejoinder. Her niece opens wide eyes of beauty, mutters '*Dio mio!*' and goes on mending an old pair of my silk stockings.

The terrible old baying voice is drawing nearer.

'Pe-pa-a! . . . Pe-e-pa-a!'

'You hear?'—Pepa is hugging herself now, and swaying from side to side in a kind of rapture.

But from the kitchen window one can see the *cancela*, its iron bars clutched by impotent hands.

'Pe-pa!'

'For the love of God—*go!*'

Pepa rises leisurely, swings and smoothes her hips. She is over forty—the hard-bitten forty of the working classes—but her hips move freely, like a girl's; her body is thin and under-nourished, but hard as iron and nearly as strong; her hair is black and heavy, and she has a lover whom she embraces nightly in the shadow of the myrtles. Consciousness of all this is in the slow movement of contempt with which she finally obeys the summons.

Encarnación's eyes follow her aunt reflectively; absently she raises her hand to touch the plumbago blossom behind her ear.

'You know, she has been very wicked to *mi tia*. If it were I, I should put a knife in her.' She makes the sign which is supposed to ward off the evil eye. 'Does not the señora find that there is something bad in old age?'

In the lassitude that envelops the Granada of today one may read the mephitic influence of the Alhambra, its spiritual triumph over the material victory of the Catholic kings. Each ashen-rose stone that has gone to build an Alhambra villa holds something of that triumph, something of that vengeance for the past: something that casts its dust over the thoughts and actions of its inhabitants and echoes grimly in the quarrels of Doña Laura and Doña Mercédes, in the savage hatred of their servants, in the hopelessness of the Alhambra maidens who set roses behind their ears to decoy the lovers who never come to snatch them from the fortress of the past.

These are the true ghosts of the Alhambra, that walk in broad daylight up and down the hill, that cluster in the twilight to listen to the nightingales whose same sweet song trembled at the lattices of their Moorish ancestors.

CHAPTER VI

NOSTALGIA

IT was the following summer that, by a lucky chance, the little carmen of Doña Mercédes came temporarily into my hands, owing to the vacation of its owner. I carried on my *negocios* from England, writing to Luisa in the Albaicin to arrange the domestic situation for me. I arrived on a day so hot that it was almost unbearable, even to such a sun-lover as myself, having spent a night in Malaga and travelled on to Granada in the morning.

At the *cancela* a little group is waiting: Luisa, with the usual miserables hanging by her petticoats; Miguel; Pepa and Encarnación, from the House of the Dead Moor; the inevitable band of nondescripts, always attracted by a new arrival; my gipsy friends, La Paca and her sister, and old Josefa.

Her face, like a witch, like a withered walnut, peers through the iron scrollwork. With a plethora of apology and circumlocution, Luisa informs me that Josefa insists upon being my house servant—and my heart sinks. I know Josefa is too old to do the work of the carmen as I would wish it done, and the vision of her ancient moth-like figure creeping about the place sends a shiver down my spine.

'It is suitable,' Luisa anxiously assures me, 'that the señora shall have a woman like Josefa on the premises. She is very old, but she is as honest as clear water; the words of the señora are to her as the tablets of stone, and she will work her fingers to the bone in the señora's service.'

Which, on the face of it, is all very fine; but I do not want anybody's fingers to be worn to the bone; I do not mind about my words being regarded as the tablets of stone—

which savours too much of responsibilities I have come hither to avoid—and I have pictured some gay and pretty creature tripping around, carolling flamenco (I hoped not too vigorously, because even an *aficionada* loses the taste for flamenco when the sorrows of the Virgin are rehearsed too often and too flamboyantly in her hearing), and contributing her carefree grace to the idyllic surroundings.

However, there is obviously nothing to be done about it for the present, and I go down to view my garden, and to make acquaintance of my impossibly romantic-looking young gardener, Manuel.

I still do not know whether all Spanish gardeners are sullen. It is a curious anomaly that English gardeners—if they are good ones—are almost invariably crabbed; they probably reserve their sweetness for their plants. Or it may be that they are permanently soured by the unaccountability of plant life, and by a climate that seems to take malicious pleasure in blasting their choicest products when these are just on the point of fruition.

However it may be, the only two sullen Andalucíans with whom I ever had acquaintance were my young Manuel, and the gardener Rafael at Malaga. Rafael was a thief, an unscrupulous bully, and (as it proved) a dangerous ruffian; whereas Manuel was merely sullen, and too grand to help beat the carpets.

He greets me unsmilingly, with forced politeness. Poor Manuel! He has been looking forward to the run of the garden throughout the summer, to the proceeds of the flower beds and the fruit trees, and he finds his plans scotched by the arrival of an Englishwoman. And, *por dios*, what an Englishwoman!—one of that intolerable kind that not only orders things to be done, but insists on their being done, not tomorrow, or some time, but *now*; and who does not scatter *duros* to sweeten the air or to make labour more endurable.

No wonder his welcome is a little sour, a little perfunctory; no wonder that when I order him briskly to make a beginning by cleaning out the swimming tank (a task which, by the look of it, has not been performed since the beginning of the century) he lowers his handsome Andalucían head and goes off to ponder on whether the game is worth the candle.

Between Josefa and Manuel a little of the gilt has vanished from the gingerbread. I send Josefa tottering to the town for wine, and Luisa, Miguel and I sit in the black-and-white tiled dining-room, discussing housekeeping. Josefa, insists Luisa, is utterly dependable; it is better I should not do my own marketing; Josefa will economize for me, and see I am not cheated.

(I learn inside of twenty-four hours that Josefa's idea of economy is to feed me on rice and a very unpleasant kind of garlic sausage; when I take the bit between my teeth and order three dozen eggs from Ana the hen-woman, she wags her grey head, and respectfully prophesies ruin for the house.)

She has, it appears, the feudal but trying habit of sleeping across my threshold. No blandishments of mine will coax her into occupying one of the several spare beds the carmen contains. 'It is not suitable, señora; I am your servant, and Doña Luisa has put you in my charge.' So I suffer the excruciating discomfort of Josefa's snores as she lies wedged between the doorposts of my doorless room. There are no doors, only curtains, inside the carmen: an arrangement which makes for coolness but denies one privacy. Josefa who, even allowing for the fact that Spanish women of the working classes are old at forty, cannot have been less than seventy years of age, lays her rheumatic bones night after night on the polished boards, with only a thin blanket to cover her. If they had been, as they are in many Spanish houses, marble tiles, there is no doubt she would have done the same.

But the stars in their courses are fighting for me. Josefa's daughter falls sick. The news is brought by one of the Albaicin scarecrows I know by sight: María, who has a litter of children, and keeps a herd of tawny goats whose milk she sells to supplement the infinitesimal earnings of her gardener husband. María comes two miles, at four in the morning, to leave a litre of the rich, sweet goats' milk at my *reja*. She shrieks like a parrot, and has a hair-raising squint, but she is a charming creature, full of gaiety and courage. Luisa has practically adopted one of her children: a boy of eight, whom she idolizes in the passionate, pathetic fashion of childless women, and spoils until a more revolting specimen of small boyhood never existed.

Josefa comes to tell me with tears that she must go to her daughter. Disconcerted, suddenly to be left without domestic services, I decide to drive up to the Albaicin and take Luisa's advice about engaging a young maid. I have actually sent for the car when a timid ring at the bell of the *cancela* sends me to reconnoitre, and between the scroll-work, peeping and bobbing like a bird, is a little face so wreathed in smiles that I can only smile back.

My blessed little Rosario! I shall always see you, prancing with excitement in your faded but spotless frock of lilac print: your little Andalucían face, which must indeed have been lovely in your youth, flashing with joyful animation, your hands fluttering like birds, your eyes brilliant with tears of gladsome anticipation.

Señora, señora—you remember me? You remember Rosario La Lavandera?'

Of course I remember her: as I remember the flat basket on which were laid, with such scrupulous and delicate care, the fruits of her labours. Never did my body linen come back without a few bouquets of sweet-smelling herbs, or a long stem of waxen *nardo* laid between the pleated folds.

'The señora is wanting a servant?'

'Oh, Rosario, do you know of someone?'

'Of whom but myself, señora? Here I am—all ready to do whatever the señora requires.'

'But the washing, Rosario— ? '

'The washing will do itself.' Indescribable is the gesture with which she consigns her former livelihood to air. 'I can come to the señora from six in the morning to nine—ten—eleven—whatever the señora pleases! I can do everything: cook, clean the house, mend, wait on the señora and look after her wardrobe—'

If I were to ask her if she could drive the car and do my typing, I am convinced she would lie nobly. She is determined to become my servant, and I am only too willing to have her. She is fifty, but hers are the lightsome movements of a girl; she is gay, wise, scrupulously cleanly in her person, honest as the day, and she has recommendations (which she begs me to take up but which I ignore) from nearly every house in the Alhambra.

Ay-di-mi! Had I known the power that lay in that humble little figure in the most spotless of print gowns, which assures me radiantly of its many virtues, and that a concensus of Granadino opinion proclaims her the best servant from La Zubia to Santa Fé, should I ever have engaged her? Yet what could seem more innocent than my Rosario, my meek little elderly handmaid, rigidly respectable, strenuously attentive, respectfully affectionate: most efficient of watchdogs who, on a summer's evening, assumed virtual control of my household?

It is about three weeks later that I awake to a suspicion that I am the victim of a system of deception, so subtle, so gentle, so artistic, that, up to the moment, I have never perceived it.

It is on the morning she places before me an object like an old washleather glove, and announces with her usual radiant satisfaction:

'There! Blessed be God, the señora has her salt, her pepper, her wine, her olives, her bread, her fruit and her *beautiful* tortilla!'

Now this tortilla reveals itself, even to a casual glance, as the most revolting, the most unworthy specimen of its kind that was ever offered in the name of food to a hungry woman. I suppose I make some pusillanimous noise of assent; Rosario withdraws, beaming, and, as I feed the tortilla in small pieces to my puppy, I begin to do some thinking.

It dawns on me that I have been eating leathery tortillas, tough goats' flesh, soapy sweetbreads, dried-up fish and indiarubber fowl without a murmur: simply because each is ushered to my table with so flowery a string of adjectives that I am obliged to accept them at their author's valuation. I have drunk inferior wine, because my Rosario assures me it is good; have meekly swallowed soups—'*muy rica, muy rica!*'—which assuredly consist of nothing but an old bone, a few grains of rice and some tepid water.

Nor does the matter rest here. I have lain upon a bed which has been 'regulated,' so I am told, 'to perfection ': only to rise in the small hours to remake it from lumpy mattress to wrinkled cover. I have accepted Rosario's assurance that the *sala* is 'as clean as a blessed altar-cloth', in spite of the fact that a book, rescued from behind the divan, comes up coated with the most loathsome detritus imaginable. I have proved all these things to be; yet, out of sheer weakness, I have gone on taking Rosario's word for it that any work of her hands is perfection, and not to be equalled throughout the whole of Granada.

It must not be supposed that she makes these claims in any spirit of vulgar boastfulness. Her face lights up, her little brown hands flutter with eagerness, her whole body stiffens with honest pride in her handiwork, after the fashion of a small child who, after many failures, presents to its teacher a faultless copy. A word of praise—and who could withhold it?—makes her vibrate with ecstasy. By sheer force of her own boundless conviction, she has succeeded in imposing on me her horrible cookery, her impressionistic house-cleaning and her hideous bed-making as the veritable masterpieces she herself truly believes them to be. At last the situation is made clear: my Rosario is an unequalled example of self-hypnosis.

The day I expose the horrible secrets of the divan I go out for six hours. On my return I am received radiantly. 'All is spotless, señora! There is not a speck of dirt to be found in any part of the house!' I am so relieved to hear the old familiar greeting that I do not so much as indicate the thick grey band of dust which a shaft of sunlight lays bare almost under my nose.

I go down to the dining-room, and she places before me two obvious bits of shoe-leather, lovingly introduced as 'a little tenderness, señora'.

I take one mouthful, lay down my knife and fork, and drawing a deep breath, am delivered of fearful heresy.

'It is hard. It is bad. It is dangerous to the stomach. I will not eat it.'

She goes as white as a blanched almond. A thousand

wrinkles appear where have been a score. She clasps her hands to her bosom, her lips begin to work helplessly.

'*Madre mia . . . madre mia de mi alma . . .*'

I have smashed a crystal palace of illusion. I have changed a creature as carefree as a sparrow to a little old woman, face to face with her own shortcomings. And it is not she, but I, who am smitten to the heart.

She waits until I have finished; then, controlling her quivering little face, she bends across the table, and with a gesture so humble that it lacerates me, touches with the tip of her finger the flowers that form its centrepiece.

I can see them as if it were yesterday: long, swinging spray of tiny cerise roses springing from a mist of plumbago; three golden coreopses, and a nameless magenta blossom like the rosettes that deck the bridles of horses in a May Day procession; and, from the heart of the bouquet, sharp like a silver scimitar, rises a waxen spray of nard.

With the only note of hesitation I have ever heard in her voice, she asks:

'But these . . . these, señora? They are good . . . these?'

Thanks be to God, the Spanish language is full of beautiful phrases of adulation; by the time I have exhausted my vocabulary the light has glimmered back into her face. She leaves me, to return with a handful of cinders in an earthenware bowl: of which, placing them at my elbow with grace a prima ballerina might envy, she murmurs, with the roucoulement of a turtle-dove:

'Your beautiful potatoes, señora!'

Is it not proof of the contrariety of the human mind that today, while enjoying a perfectly cooked meal, I should remember with wistfulness a soft voice at my elbow: 'A little tenderness, daughter of my soul?'

Her housekeeping was masterly; no one ever found the youngest and sweetest fruits and vegetables as unerringly as Rosario, no one was such an expert judge of the young goats and poultry that her cooking reduced to offal! No woman in the fishmarket ever made an unlawful *perrachica* out of Rosario's shopping, from which it was her pride to render me as much change as possible from the *duros* with which she was provided. Her laundry work was exquisite, her mending like the fine threads of a spider. Was it her fault that she did not combine all the culinary virtues with these?

So the young Carmen comes to end these difficulties: a bouncing damsel of fifteen, with a rose eternally behind her ear and a string of beaux who take turns at the *reja* in the evening; with a rattling soprano voice and an inexhaustible repertory of flamenco which Rosario, at my orders, keeps within due bounds. She has been trained in a more sophisticated household than those with which Rosario was familiar. I am waited on, maided and spoilt as only Spanish servants are capable of spoiling one. I am heavily chaperoned. Certain of my visitors are sent to the *reja;* one or two, who do not pass Rosario's exigent standard, are not even allowed in the garden.

To wake up in the roseate Granada dawn; to step out on a balcony overhanging the Vega like an eagle's nest; to watch the twin bells of the little convent at the foot of the hill performing their grave head-over-heels dance like a pair of tumbler pigeons; to see the golden lichen on the roofs turning to orange in the sunrise, and the *sierras* flaming like a tulip bed across the rose-pink plain; to see Rosario moving slowly and gently between the flower patches, snipping here a rose, here a spray of frail plumbago or a fleshy golden marigold to compose the bouquets she arranges with such grace and delight, or to watch her sitting on the wall, humming softly, scouring the copper vessels with lemon peel, or coming from the swimming tank with the great stone jars of water balanced on her head—these are pleasures for which, if they never come again, I give thanks day by day.

The round tub is placed out of doors, on red bricks that never lose their warmth of centuries of sun; the down-dropping clusters of wistaria overhead make a pattern of cool shadow and—even at this early hour of the morning—burning light.

Lorenzo is tugging on the corner of the towel Rosario carries on her arm—Lorenzo, the size of a coconut and nearly as round: jetty black, with preternaturally loving eyes and a thousand melting tricks. They say Spaniards do not care for animals; if ever a puppy was loved and spoiled by the household, it is my Lorenzo.

The bath is the beginning of his day, when he squeals round my toes, makes grinning dashes at the soap and yaps wildly at Rosario, as she lifts the great stone *olla*, and pours the ice-cold Alhambra water over my head. He buries his little black muzzle in the bowl of milk, while, out in the sun, Rosario serves breakfast—the deep basin of coffee, the fresh *bollos*, the lovely dairy butter and heaped bowl of peaches and grapes. (I forget, on my return to England, that one does not help oneself to an entire bunch of grapes, and munch it lusciously, with the juice trickling down one's chin.) By half-past seven breakfast is finished, and the morning's work begins.

By eleven o'clock, fingers are sagging on the typewriter, head is heavy, the heat has begun to invade the house, which with the lowering of the *persanas*, becomes a tank, filled with pale green light. Rosario, a little pale, a little damp from her long, steep journey to the market and back, arrives with her loaded basket of the morning's shoppings—always to scold me for too much money spent on stamps and tobacco.

'I'm going up to the Alhambra now, Rosario. I may be back at twelve. There may be people for lunch.'

'The house is the señora's. It is for her to command.'

'I may be back at twelve . . .' she can neither read nor write, nor can she tell the time by the clock; the sun is her clock, and I have not known it to fail her.

In the shadowed *patios* of the Alhambra the jet of a little fountain cools one's wrists; from the broad stone embrasure of a window the exquisite, pale, brilliant landscape dazzles the eyes. The rhythm and tempo of Andalucía enters into one, so that haste becomes folly and a too-sudden gesture an indiscretion to be avoided.

Sometimes there is amusing company at the casa di Apolonio, the little tavern built in the Alhambra precincts, whose upper floor is inhabited by the family of Angel Barrios, the composer On Sunday mornings friends and pupils gather there; there is music, singing and someone recites his poems; if it is Sunday, one gravitates to 'Apolonio's' house as a matter of course.

The tavern is patronized by all kinds—by a few (happily very few) tourists from the Alhambra pensions, by the young bullfighters who take the walk up the hill as part of their training, by countrymen, *commerciantes* and priests. The countrymen leave their little black asses tied up to the *rejas* and lean on the counter, drinking *aguardiente*, which is a raw, fiery cognac, very unpleasant to the refined taste. Many wear cummerbunds of red cloth round their middles, which serve the double purpose of purse and luncheon basket. I am always offered a piece of the tortilla brought from this unhygienic storage-place, and have learned how to preserve the amenities by explaining that tortilla does not agree with me. Lorenzo, sprawling on the counter, saves the situation by eating bits of tortilla, drinking quite as much *tinto* as is good for him, and ends by falling into a drunken sleep on my knees.

The conversation is always a delight, for the language of the peasants is a language of poetry and philosophy; they delight in images, in long, abstract discussions which seem to have started with sunrise, and will surely last until the sun goes down. The clipped, bastard argot of the bull-fighters sounds among these almost as foreign as the *madrileño* Spanish of the priests who come in the striped cotton pyjamas which seem to be the accepted négligé of the granadino to take their glasses of manzanilla before their midday sleep.

Lunch is over. Stretched naked between linen sheets, the flies banished temporarily by Rosario's operations with the Flit gun—'el Flee,' as, with the Andalucían custom of dropping final consonants, she calls it—sleep blots out consciousness of the by now overpowering heat.

Rosario insists upon 'the five o'clock': not very English tea, but as I am no connoisseur of tea, and only keep it for visitors, I accept her tribute to my nationality, usually disposing of it tactfully through the *reja* and, presently, ringing for sherry.

The light in the garden has altered; the shadows of the cypresses lie the other way, and the handsome, sullen Manuel is flooding the little trenches with water and languidly spraying the roses. On nights of fiesta he will be hanging the Chinese lanterns in the trees, and arranging the chairs on the terrace from which we look down upon star-scattered Granada.

The two servants sit by the well, Rosario mending the linen or darning stockings while Carmen reads aloud, slowly and laboriously, following each word with her finger—from the children's story books in words of one syllable which represent the sum of her learning; even so, she sometimes comes to ask me a word. It is a kind of Spanish *Babes in the Wood*, and is taken in the most serious fashion; from the *reja* I can hear long, murmuring discussions of characters and motives, which go on for an hour after Carmen has finished her reading. I like these evening gatherings about the well, which are sometimes swelled by Pepa and Encarnación from the Dead Moor; the snatches of song, the long ripple of gossip—as I like the days when they wash out their body linen, scrubbing it on the stone margin of the well, or wash their beautiful black hair, and sit in the sun to dry and then oil it. All their occupations have a peacefulness, a simplicity, a flavour of tradition, like the Andaluz dialect they talk. I am glad to record how much of my happiness in Granada I owe to my servants.

A drowsy lizard darts into the sprouting hart's tongue fern, as I balance on the warm brick edge of the Moorish swimming tank—now, thanks to Manuel's unsmiling efforts, clear as crystal. Cold as ice the water that receives one's grateful limbs. Frogs and goldfish scatter before the few lazy strokes that carry one to the farther end. A dappling of yellow sunset and green reflections lies on the deep water. Already the sun is slipping swiftly towards the empurpled rim of the Vega. The end of another peaceful day.

Rosario has filled my little bedroom with the light of a dozen candles. Already the blue night presses on the *rejas*. Rosario stands beaming, with my fresh linen across her arms.

'The señora has company tonight?'

'No. Order a car. I shall go up to the Albaicin.'

The ghost of a frown appears on my henchwoman's brow; the slow movements of the hairbrush are suspended.

'It is as the señora pleases . . . Why does the señora go always to that bad place? To be sure, the house of Doña Luisa is all that is good, when one gets there; but there are many bad people. It is not safe for the señora!'

How to explain to my conventional little Rosario that, after the tender demureness of the carmen, its isolated quietude, there is something astringent, something stimulating in that curious, savage world up the opposite hill? I have even gone there on foot, and never suffered molestation. I am known to most of that shifty population by sight, and, shifty or not, have never encountered anything but courtesies. And it is an experience to remember—that lonely climb between mouldering façades blazoned with moonlight, through alleys I can touch on either side with my outstretched arms, past dark *rejas* from which comes the murmured '*Buena' noche*' of some invisible friend. It is not a mile from the heart of the town to the calle de la Parra— the street of the Vines; to the Villa Luisa, to laughter and singing, perhaps to some gusty drama that threatens to settle itself with knives, and then gets absorbed into the atmosphere of goodwill.

And then, at midnight, or later, the car returns; I am driven back—from one world into another: I exchange the turbulence of the Albaicin for the dreamless quiet, threaded with nightingale song, of the Alhambra. This, for periods covering three happy years, is a Granada day.

CHAPTER VII

THE HOT DAYS

IT is August. We have had several weeks of scorching heat: Granada simmers, the plains and the lower hillsides are burnt to the colour of an old and mangy lion; even we on the Alhambra hill suffer, our tempers shorten, and a surly disinclination for company drives us to avoid our friends. For twenty-four hours we have had *la tormenta*, a local version of sirocco, the hot wind which, blowing from the African desert, brings with it always a wave of petty crime. Pepa goes about with the face of a witch, Encarnación and Carmen are walking thunderstorms: even my little Rosario's brow is puckered with puzzled fretfulness. On the Campo de los Martires the heat meets one like the blast of a furnace; one uses one's fan, and beats the suffocating air more stiflingly into one's lungs.

Diego and I descend to the dungeons which, in other days, harboured the captured Moors, one of which is now converted into a squalid little tavern, whose one virtue is that it affords a refuge cold and damp as a well. The drinking-vessels are fearful; Diego chivalrously rinses one for me in a newly drawn bucket of well-water and polishes it with his spotless handkerchief. The proprietor takes no notice. Like everyone else, he has *la murria*—the black dog on his shoulder. The coins we toss on the counter fail to rouse his interest; he lets them lie. We drink a vile *tinto*—which might as appropriately be called *tinta* (ink), but which has at least the merit of icy coldness.

'It is too hot here for you: you should go to the sea. Or perhaps to the mountains. I have an idea! I will combine with a friend of mine, if you like, who has a house in the *sierra . . .*'

I know, however, too much about Diego's 'combinations' to lend myself to his idea, but the word *sierra*, implanted in my consciousness, raises a tantalizing vision of refreshment.

At night, when we all recline in rocking-chairs under the quinces—

'Luisa', I say. 'I want to go to the *sierra*.'

Luisa is enchanted; Miguel also. We will make a party— as big a party as will go in Pedro's big car! Climatic conditions excuse, I hope, the terseness with which I veto this bright suggestion. Not for a fortune will I be crowded into a car, large or small, with a lot of other people, when the mere contact of one's own flesh is all but unbearable.

Foiled in her intention of giving her friends a free outing, there are almost tears in Luisa's voice as she protests.

'But we must have music! There must be singing!'

'Certainly there must be singing. We will take Manuel.'

'*Por dios, Manuel! Oiga, hombre: no tiendras miedo?*'

The blind man, gently and patiently waiting the command to tune his instrument, turns his head like a faded El Greco towards our voices with a sweet, doubtful smile.

'We will have a chicken in the pot,' exults Luisa, 'and much wine—no? And the Manchego cheese that is the señora's favourite and our own grapes and some Trevéllez ham and the little sausages. . . .'

The party, when it assembles, is wildly enthusiastic. In spite of my prohibition, several unauthorized persons have managed to attach themselves, and stand smiling, with modest confidence, around Pedro's big car, which indeed is big enough to accommodate a dozen—according to Andalucían standards of hospitality and conviviality. Unfortunately, I am not feeling in the least Andalucían; I want nothing but air, space and freedom from any sort of social obligation.

The company manifests polite interest in my long blue slacks and white shirt—my first, and, it may be added, my only departure from Granadino convention. For today, at least, I must lay aside the discreet, long-sleeved dark gown, the *velo* and the gloves which, in order not to embarrass my friends, I assume for my walks abroad.

With that instinct amounting to genius for wearing the right clothes on the wrong occasion, Luisa has chosen to appear in her best black *Crêpe de chine* with frills (frills are a disease this year in Granada), an elegant black shaven lamb coat (gift of her patron, the marchesa)—and a pair of white kid beach sandals. How she supports the ensemble is a mystery bound up in the unfathomable depths of her vanity.

It is now my business to prune off the uninvited units of the party. Luisa (who is, of course, responsible for their presence) is loud in deprecation of the attempted abuse of the señora's well-known generosity; but when it comes to separating her from her horrible small protégé, Antonio, the son of one-eyed María la Cabrera (obviously dressed up for the occasion in a new white sailor suit, and smirking with confidence of his welcome), the tune changes. It is cutting off her hands, gouging out her eyes, making mincemeat of her heart to leave behind the little king of her soul. While the king of Luisa's soul wriggles and spits and makes to clamber into the car without further ado, I capture him by the slack of his knickers and cold-bloodedly inform Luisa that I am prepared to perform all of these unpleasant operations, rather than take Antonio into the *sierras:* in which decision I am most surprisingly supported by Antonio's mother, who snatches her offspring, gives him a few all too tender cuffs, and, with unusual spirit, informs Luisa that 'she told her so'. At this defiance of her supreme authority, Luisa's eyes become for a moment diabolical; at the next, her smile flashes out, and she steps as lightsomely into the car as though there had never been any argument.

The only extra person retained is the gipsy boy, Pablo, who is to look after Manuel, and see that he does not come to grief when we get into the mountains. Humble and deferential, with manners like velvet, he gets up beside the chauffeur; Miguel, Manuel and I dispose ourselves in the interior, and the assembled company waves us off with as much emotion as if we were leaving for another star.

We seem at first to be pushing our way through a solid wall of heat. Leaving the cauldron of the town, we proceed— always at a terrifying pace—towards the foothills, the low, lava-like slopes that summer has reduced to ash-heaps. The lion-coloured plain is now bleached to a pallor of sand, and the yet early morning sun spreads a shimmering haze over all the foreground. Above us, silver border to a sky hard and bright as enamel, are the eternal snows. At 'The Last Inn' we pause for refreshment; we collect, at my suggestion, a big stone jar of Avellano water, which proves a godsend through the first sweltering stages of the ascent.

Bit by bit, the astonishing Andalucían landscape unrolls itself, as we climb a broad, precipitous road; the lower hills which form the background to Granada have the appearance of old hessian curtains, bunched together and spread out fan-wise at their bases, in heavy folds vaguely tufted with the black wild olives. The pale, distant Vega, that always, at dawn and at night, has some strange shifting quality that makes of it neither land nor water, lies smooth as an inland sea between our heights and the crusted ridge of the more distant mountains, and above us, always, are the unchallenged peaks, with patches of snow spread out, as Miguel says, 'like linen upon a giant's drying ground'.

We look down dizzily upon villages, pinned in the clefts of ravines into which an eagle launches itself from some splintered edge, and vanishes as though sucked by an air current into the abyss. At such a moment, when all of one's conscious being is drawn into the nerves of sight, one becomes poignantly aware of the blind man, sitting patiently, lost in his darkness, unable to conceive a scene which he has never known.

I start to try and tell Manuel something of what we are seeing; he smiles sweetly, but without conviction. How should he respond to words which, for him, hold no meaning? What is blue, what is white, what is sand-coloured, to the consciousness of a blind man? In foolish pain for one to whom there is nothing painful in his infirmity, I seek for something that shall bring within the focus of his understanding our fantastic environment, and find it in the masses of lavender which suddenly line our way.

The perfume of the rich, violet spires—so much deeper in colour and in scent than the English variety—comes in gusts through the open windows, mingled with that of the wild thyme and rosemary that grow in low clumps close to the earth. I stop the car and tear up handfuls, which I press into Manuel's hands, bidding him smell. His thin hands of ivory, with beautiful bones, lift the nosegay to his face; a look of astonishment—less for the beauty of the perfume than for its difference from all the odours to which he is accustomed: the Albaicin odours of rancid oil, of dung, of goats' and asses' and human bodies—dawns upon his pale, humiliated face. I look hastily at a thin bushy plant that resembles love-in-a-mist without its blossoms, and is spangled on every stem and leaf with ladybirds.

The air is still very hot, but we give a shout as the car swings round a bend into shadow, and brings us to the first of the snows. We yell to the driver to stop; Miguel and I leap out, to bury our bare arms to the shoulder in the icy drift. We hurl snowballs at each other, until the polite astonishment of the rest turns us self-conscious, and we return rather sheepishly to the car, and to Luisa, who clearly, though courteously, regards us as mad.

A little higher up, close to a partly built mountain hostel which (like many things in Andalucía) will probably never be completed, we come upon a cave, which is a shepherds' tavern. The proprietor is a genial fellow, delighted to welcome us; we are the first human beings he has seen for days, as the workmen from the hostel are on strike, and the sheep are 'over the other side'—whatever that may mean. We crowd into the cave, tenderly surrounding Manuel and his guitar: we order 'the best wine', which, to my surprise, is very good indeed when it comes.

'*La musica! La musica!*'

Led with enthusiasm by the tavern-keeper, we encourage Manuel by beating out a rhythm with our hands, but he is very nervous. All the sensitiveness of the blind makes him conscious of this strange, separate world; he feels the mountains he cannot see, he senses the awful remoteness from his familiar, crowded Albaicin. It takes a great deal of wine to make him respond to our solicitations, though his fingers test delicately the effect of the elevation, of the thin, rarefied air, which makes us all a little breathless, on his guitar. And at last the attenuated thread of his voice mounts up, he launches his frail cadenza.

By this time, the wine is in all our heads, and, although wine is said to blunt the perceptions, I became aware of a thing I had not previously noticed: that, of all our little party, Miguel and I are the only two wholly happy and at our ease. The others are nervous in varying degrees: Luisa snappily so, Pablo and the driver quiet and 'edgey'. The deep black eyes of Pablo are blank with resignation, the driver hunches his shoulders, gulps his wine and has the air of going quietly towards certain martyrdom. I take an opportunity of commenting on it, quietly, with Miguel. His response is characteristic.

'*Claro!* They have none of them been in the mountains before. And as for Luisa—is she not always unhappy when she is in the presence of something which she is obliged to recognize as greater than herself?' he replies, with the alarming psychological insight which, on several occasions, I have already surprised in him.

'It doesn't say much for the success of my party!'

'*Qué disparate!* So long as we enjoy ourselves, what do the others matter?' says Miguel blandly.

We make our farewells, promising to look in on the way down, and from now on the ascent is formidable. For the last few kilometres the vegetation has been diminishing in height and quantity, and now is almost Alpine in character. Small, star-like plants, like frost formations, are pressed close to the earth, silvering its barren surfaces. The rancour of the rocks has given way to an upward-soaring grandeur. The snow is creeping down towards us; the air is delicately fresh, but still not cold.

Luisa's face is thin and sullen; her lips are a bitter grey line across her beautiful square teeth. To make a diversion, Miguel starts to sing, then encourages the gipsy boy to sing in Calo, which brings a pale smile to Manuel's lips. In return for the compliment, I sing *Fair Daffodils*, whose rhythm and intervals leave the audience politely puzzled. This brings us round several awkward corners, where

Luisa shows a disposition to shriek and clutch my arm. Resisting an inclination to box her ears, I whisper to her to behave herself, and not frighten Manuel, who is very grey and quiet.

Actually, there is nothing to jest about in this part of the journey; no longer broad and relatively well-surfaced, the road has dwindled to a shaly track, barely wide enough to accommodate the wheel-base. We lurch over miniature boulders in low gear—for even the high spirits of an Andalucían driver are reduced by the possibility of a six hundred feet slither to eternity. On one side is sheer rock face, on the other a dizzying slope of shale, that plunges from a crumbling edge down to the valley—which, from this height, resembles a fine needlework pattern, executed on stretched plush.

A group of labourers are repairing the track, and look up sullenly as the car approaches. They show no disposition to get out of our way, or to shift the boulders which make it impossible for us to continue further, for, in their eyes, anyone who comes into the mountains in a car is a capitalist, and a grinder of the faces of the poor.

It is painful to relate that the three able-bodied men we have as escort show no taste for coping with the situation: that it takes British arrogance, enforced by a ringing British accent, to win us our passage. 'Take care: offer them money!' whispers Luisa, trying to prevent me from opening the door. 'Offer them *what*?'—I know what, if I were a man, I should offer these glowering Catalans; but, being what is erroneously called 'a poor, weak woman', I descend, to employ my only weapon, the thin edge of a well-tested tongue; and, after a rather queasy minute or two, a few boulders are sullenly heaved aside—as little aside as possible, so that the car just, and only just, manages to lurch past.

I am rather cold with Miguel on returning to the car: his only contribution to the situation being the thoughtful remark that it is, perhaps, a pity we have to return the same way.

Across a small, green valley, which is a mere cup in the snowy crests that still tower above our heads runs a snow stream, to empty itself into a black little lake. The sun is blazing, and our first action is to bury the wine in the snow. Luisa gets out, and stands like a moulting hen, loathing her surroundings. Following our instructions, Pablo leads Manuel, very carefully and gently, to some little caves, where he will be sheltered from the wind, if it rises; and Miguel and I hurl ourselves at the snows and proceed on foot to scale the last peak, from which he promises me a sight of the African mountains.

Alas, the day is not clear enough; but from that altitude of snow, which clutches our bare ankles, and makes powdery whiteness up to the knees of our slacks, we look down through dizzying space, through trails of flying cloud, upon what now amounts to a toy range of mountains, and so stand silent, to receive the benediction of solitude.

On descending, we find Luisa still doing her broody hen act, in almost exactly the same spot upon which we left her: although she has the grace to flash into a pale reflection of her usual smile as I run up to her.

'*Pues*, Luisa—! Why isn't the food unpacked? Where are the others? They must be perishing of hunger.'

'Is it for me to sit in a cave, alone with those people? As for following you up the mountain—*madre mia*, what a terrible place this is! We shall not be staying long? The señora knows I should not be neglecting my business!'

'You'll forget all about that when you've had your *almuerzo*', I assure her, with more hope than conviction.

There is no doubt my party is going bad on me, but I refuse to be depressed. Miguel, who shares my sentiments, now becomes very exhibitionistic, performs antics in the snow, terrifies Luisa by pretending he is going to fling himself into the lake, and grins wickedly at me for support and admiration. Feeling like the *dompteur* of a circus troupe, whose animals have got out of hand, I sharply order him to unpack the wine from its snow bed, and go to find the others, who are huddled in the cave, stricken into apparent paralysis of limbs and speec horgans by their environment. Pablo, whose eyes are closed, has gone a sick green; the chauffeur is moodily chewing a cigarette with an ir of only waiting for the worst, and Manuel strikes me to the heart by his resemblance to the dead Count of Orgáz. He smiles faintly and patiently at the sound of my voice, and I hurriedly distribute food, hoping this will create the right sort of diversion.

The scene is of incredible beauty. A light wind has risen, and sends black ripples, each crested with a thin silver rim, across the dark little lake. Shreds of mist go scudding down the valley; they pass us like floating veils of confirmation, although, from Luisa's shuddering withdrawal, they might be witches' cobwebs. Yet there is nothing witch-like about these heights, as there is in some of the more seaward ranges of the *sierras:* there is some curious integrity and purity of aspiration in these heavenward-reaching peaks, that fill one with a vast contentment, as simple as the happiness of childhood.

While we devour our chicken, of which everyone, with mute accord, presses the largest and tenderest portions into the blind man's hand, a flock of sheep comes over the shoulder of the nearest hill, followed by two tall, Biblical figures in sheepskins, with sandals of hide thonged on to their bare feet, which, like all the exposed parts of their bodies, are burnt to a Moorish darkness. In their battered faces, their eyes have the pale, startling glare of the eyes of goats.

True to the traditions of Andalucían hospitality, we invite them to join our repast; they accept, simply, correctly, laying their crooks across the entrance to the cave and modestly taking the outer places. They are very shy—too shy to talk—and it presently transpires that they have never seen a foreign woman before.

The food, as I expected, has restored the spirits of the party, and we all start to sing *fandanguillos.* Suddenly one of the shepherds raises his arm to point.

'*Ya viene agua!*'

Almost before the words are spoken, our hollow is drenched with rain, which blows horizontally across the surface of the earth: the little stream begins to boil, the lake looks as though a million spears were hurled into it, the sun goes in and we have the first intimation of mountain cold.

Luisa, who has the advantage of us all in her fur coat, now makes the most of her discomfort, which Miguel and I profess rather grandly to ignore, having much less on than the other members of our party. She exaggerates the chattering of her teeth, and her eyes, like the eyes of an ill-used monkey, accuse me of brutality, in letting her in for such an experience. Presently she reproaches me with cruelty to Manuel, who is bearing the cold with saint-like patience, thinking only of his guitar, which he covers with his tattered coat. Something of a situation starts to develop in the cave, in which I feel that Miguel is the only one wholly on my side. I remind Luisa, with a touch of acrimony, that it was only owing to my insistence that she had not forced her friends into this expedition. Courtesy reaches as low an ebb as it is ever allowed to do in Andalucía.

The rain, however, soon passes, and feeling that, on Manuel's account, it is not wise to linger, I organize our return to the car; whereupon Luisa suddenly becomes radiant, tells everyone that the mountains are a miracle, that she would have given her life, rather than have missed such an experience, that her friends will be mad with jealousy when she tells them about it—and we find ourselves cautiously descending towards the spot where we left the roadmenders.

'They have gone, haven't they, Miguel?'

'Certainly they have gone; nobody is there.'

The rocks are on our right, the plunging chasm of shale on our left, and we are in second gear, moving, perhaps, just a little too fast for absolute safety . . .

Miguel sees it first.

He has just time to yell to the driver, and I to clap my hand over Luisa's mouth to strangle her shriek. We see the gipsy cower. The driver must be intelligent, and quicker in his reactions than the average Andalucían peasant, for he cannot possibly have seen what Miguel and I see: the two-ton boulder that crashes down from our right, and vanishes with the impetus of its own weight into the chasm within a yard of the bonnet of the car.

We skid a little—a very little—as the brakes go on and I, on the left, the outside edge, feel our back wheel subside just that fraction which, on such a surface, might mean the end for us all. The gipsy boy moans, and we hear the driver's grunt, as the thrust of low gear against the brake drags us out of our predicament—none too soon. A clod of earth follows the boulder, and, through the back window, as we go on, I see, on the heights from which the boulder came, a head, quickly raised, and as quickly lowered.

It takes a lot of wine at the shepherds' tavern to restore us after that. Pablo is nearly fainting when we pull him from his seat and thrust a glass of wine into his hand, and Luisa, for the first and only time in the years I have known her, is reduced to speechlessness.

The heat rises to meet us as we drop down the mountain. Our heads and ears are drumming; presently my nose starts to bleed, and I am obliged to get out, and bleed comfortably and discreetly into the lavender. The sun is blazing down the sky; it is the hour for watering the gardens.

The blind man sleeps, with a look of beatitude on his face. Soon he will be back in his crowded Albaicin, back from the fearsome silence into heartening clamour—the clop, the clatter, the jingle which make up the texture of his existence. He will tune his guitar to the loud, familiar voices that give him the confidence of which, in those remote and soundless regions, he felt himself bereft. He has been too near eternity—an eternity outside the scope of his slender mysticism—for the comfort of his soul. So he dreams of the paradise of the Albaicin, of singing under the vines.

And with every foot we drop, the blood beats faster in Luisa's veins; the colour rushes back to her soft, olive cheek, the sparkle to her eyes; she is more voluble in her expressions of ravishment and joy in her recent adventure, she commands us to remember how she played in the snow like a child—and how it was she who started us singing when we were afraid, *por dios*, yes, afraid of the grandeur of the mountains! Yes, it is she who has truly the character of the mountains within her . . . and so forth and so on, in the old familiar vein: while, within that little, perfect head, race the thoughts of her house, of her tavern, of the people who perhaps have been robbing her, of the stupidity and carelessness of her servants, of the madness of neglecting her business for a whole day. . . .

And so we race into Granada; we take the Puerta Real on two wheels, we roar up the Reyes Católicas with a blasting of horns, we swing into the calle Goméres at an angle which flings us all pell-mell, and draws a shriek of delight from Luisa, who adores a circus turn like that, and groan at last on to the Campo de los Martires.

It has not yet started to be cool, and the elms hold the heat down like a green tent; but the evening light is exquisite, after the glitter of the snows.

'Goodnight, and thank you,' says Miguel; he holds out his hand, smiles, and sighs. 'For a day like this one lives better—no?'

CHAPTER VIII

THE COLD DAYS

W E sit over the brasero in my room, which is full of the fumes of charcoal and tobacco. It has been like this for a week, and there is no reason why it should not go on in the same way for another week, or longer, because the window opening on to the balcony is warped with the gales, and you have to choose between smashing the glass or staying sealed up, like a moth in the killing bottle, until the sun comes out again to shrink the wood.

Now and again we set the door open on the stairwell, and clouds of cigarette smoke go wreathing down into the humid depths, and hang about in faint bluish trails for an hour or more afterwards. The after-odour of *canarios* is not agreeable, and we have come to the end of the fine contraband tobacco one buys in little tissue-paper bundles from the bakery. The baker's wife looks up and down the street before slipping her hand under the counter, and sometimes, if the bread is not rising properly, or her husband's dyspepsia makes him ill-tempered, she will swear she has not got, has never had, any tobacco at all.

It is not a cheerful house, nor a cheerful room. Tottering on the edge of the Alhambra hill, there is not a wall that does not crumble to the touch, that has not wide cracks of earthquake sprawling like spiders' legs across the plaster; and because no wall stands plumb, and no floor even, the oddments of furniture lean out at freakish angles, swing or bow towards one with the banging of a door, or with the too robust, too lively bound of the little servant on the stairs. Lying in that ramshackle bed, I have, as a matter of fact, seen an enormous chest swing out and crash on its

83

face on the floor; but that was earthquake, and this is not the earthquake season. Yet this House of the Dead Moor trembles and shrinks from every blast that slams the dead boughs of wistaria against the lower windows, and converts the palms into scourges wielded by some giant and maniac hand.

All the streams of the Alhambra clatter with the overflow from the snows; the sound of running water is woven into one's dreams. One day, when some waste pipe or culvert burst, it converts the lower rooms into a raging torrent, which subsides to leave a wilderness of mud, in which one gropes for letters, guitar strings and such trifles as have been wafted from the tables by the draughts.

For all the centuries that Granada has carried its burden of snows, of gales, of rains that wash away the very roofs from over the heads of its inhabitants, no provision has grown up that affords even a modicum of comfort during the vicious winter months. There are no chimneys that do not smoke—as one knows who has suffered the asphyxiating smoke of olive-wood fires; no shutters that keep out the wind, no adequate coverings for the cold stone floors.

Resignedly, the Granadina takes down from her walls the great brasero bowls which, polished to a brightness of gold, furnish their shining summer adornment; lays across them the handful of dried twigs to which she sets light, and patiently sets to work with a palm leaf fan, until the smoke disperses, the flames die down, and a heap of white ash with fire at its heart remains to be moulded with a little iron spade into a neat crater. This she places beneath the table, whose voluminous cloth preserves the vortex of warmth, towards which the household gravitates as naturally as the English household towards the hearth. With knees, calves and ankles pleasantly toasting, the stoic company rests its elbows on the table, drinks *aguardiente*, and tries, by huddling its shoulders into shawls and capes, to pretend it is not perishing of cold.

In the better class houses there is some sort of central heating, which functions feebly, one might say reluctantly, or blazes like a fiery furnace, emitting blood-curdling noises: either of which conditions the householder is apt to accept as an Act of God, and rarely troubles to ameliorate. Taken as a whole, the Granadino is economical—to avoid a harsher term—even where his personal comfort is concerned; he is also profoundly languid, with the languor of in-breeding, of an exhausted stock and of the *Weltschmerz* which lies heavy upon the town. Exactly as the Andalucían peasant chooses, on the whole, to exist upon the minimum necessary to keep life in his body, rather than to commit himself to organized labour, so will the Granadino prefer to risk the dread *pulmonía*, which takes its toll every winter among the lowered vitalities of the inhabitants, than to take active measures to improve his living conditions.

The fortitude of the Granadino to his barbarous winter is understandable, when one reflects that the first ray of sunshine, the first hint of balminess in the air, the first bud that breaks upon the spraying rose banishes, not merely the actuality, but the memory of his discomforts. With sublime forgetfulness of the misery of, perhaps, half an hour ago, he emerges, to sun himself on the streets, to launch his crusted witticisms, while the women rear their glossy heads and push back the sodden *velo* that is tucked into the shabby little fur collars on their winter coats.

El piropo revives, as abruptly as a jaded plant under a jet of water: *el piropo*, which is the spice of the promenade— the bold yet subtle glance, the whispered '*Guapa!*' the measured pursuit and the murmured phrase that combines flattery, humour and obscenity in a fashion only to be achieved by the Andalucían. *El piropo* flourishes only in the sun; under the low grey winter sky gallantry perishes, like the green buds of Spring.

'Let's go down to the house of the widow of Pelaiz and have some manzanilla.'

So we put on our thick, sensible, English clothing; I have blushed for being so comfortably clad in those Granadino winters. We lurch and slither under the elms, and the clamour of the water is too loud for conversation; the leafless boughs shower drops like leaden pellets on our heads, and from the ancient, rose-ashen walls the fountains come crashing, as though the Alhambra itself has become a vast reservoir, that threatens to engulf the town in its volume of water. The Vega is blotted out in purple-blue, the mountains flattened under their burden of rain-sodden cloud.

In the calle de Goméres, the few human beings we meet look like bedraggled birds, the women pitiful in their thin, shoddily smart coats, their pretentious little shoes of patent leather. The men fare better in the handsome Andalucían capes of heavy, expensive cloth, faced with crimson or green or dark brown plush, which forms a collar when it is flung in the correct fashion over the shoulder. No matter how faded or antique a cape may be, it has a dignity which is enhanced by the Cordobés hat which accompanies it. But the rain drips off the wide brims of the Cordobéses and the faces beneath them are purplish-yellow with discomfort. A little clutch of Alhambra beggars, pressed close under the stone arch, as though stone itself were less pitiless than the continual downpour of cold rain, look like nothing so much as bundles of rags, hung up to drip.

To add to the almost intolerable misery of the scene, this is the season of funerals. At all hours of the day one meets the black processions mounting the Alhambra hill—from the opulent motor hearses and following cars of the rich middle classes, to the tragic little groups that, lacking the money even to buy mourning—and what can more publicly signallize one's indigence in a Latin country?—bear among themselves the thin wooden shell containing some remnant of humanity, more to be envied than pitied for its escape from 'the wound of living'. Sometimes the burden is no more than a little cardboard box, carried under a father's arm, while the other arm supports the woman whose bowed head conceals her grief and her shame.

There is red mud up to our shoe-tops and our ankles are soaked when, with collars turned up and hands thrust into the pockets of our British Burberrys, we tramp down the Zacatin, turn into one of its narrowest alleys, and enter the house of the widow of Pelaiz—a tavern so blessedly obscure that it is ignored, even during the summer season, by the tourists.

A painted canvas screen divides the bar into two sections —supposedly first and second class; it might be effective if one ever knew which was which. Behind the bar are the black, distended goatskins, the bullfight posters and the dark casks of sherry. The ceiling, which has 'toned' to a deep caramel colour, is decorated with Angelica-Kauffman-like entwinements of roses and ribbons and musical instruments. It has been like that for a century, although, probably, to begin with, the caramel patine was cream, or even white.

The electric light is very poor, because the whole town is using it; it makes the men's faces yellow and brings up all the lines and hollows in deep black, like a wood-cut. There are glasses of *vino tinto* and plates of anchovies and olives all the way along the counter, and the guides, who live on cigarettes and alcohol through the winter, are leaning up against the counter, letting their teeth chatter. Somebody must be paying. The place is dark, and smells of wet clothes and starvation.

We pay a round of drinks and go into the parlour, where a crimson tablecloth conceals the ripe, red, glowing brasero, of whose heat our frozen shins take comfort; it is a privilege accorded only to 'distinguished patrons'. It is all uncannily quiet; no one is talking. Now and again a draught slices across the room as the street door opens.

When our glasses are empty for the third or fourth time, we get up and go out into the Reyes Católicos, and the whole pavement is arrow-points of rain, and the gutters foaming brown. The beggars have vanished under their cones of sodden newspaper, and the goods in the shop windows are obliterated by the water that courses in sheets down the plate glass. Two nuns go by, under umbrellas; their wet habits cling to their legs, and make them stumble.

Trini's tavern in the Manigua is not a polite tavern, although, in comparison with the house of the widow of Pelaiz, it is a veritable palace, with its broad white patio, its spotless marble tables and bracketed aspidistras, that lend a greenhouse aspect to the walls. The rain is cascading into the *patio*, and the chairs are stacked up under the gallery. The paving is afloat with mud and water.

We stop in the glittering little bar, where Trinidad herself, black as thundercloud, her vicious old face made villainous by a single protruding tusk and by the piled-up masses of her improbable black hair, receives us as though our arrival were the one thing needed to make the morning wholly intolerable. We know our Trini, and take no notice. The bar is bright with glass and chromium, and there is a little daylight, that lies like a wet grey film over the polished surfaces, and excuses Trini's parsimony in electricity. The rain in the patio drowns conversation. We order manzanilla.

The girls from the neighbouring houses come in, with woollen shawls over their thin silk dresses, and tease Trini for plates of her soup; they smell of *Quelques Fleurs* perfume, and the smell of the soup and the cognac and the perfume belongs to the cold days, like the little red noses of the girls and the powder and lipstick that stares off their chilled faces, and their look of bewilderment and suspended animation. For there is no 'business' worth speaking of in the cold days, which freeze men's senses as well as their bodies, and drive them for sheer warmth to their lawful bed mates.

After Trini's there is the Trente-Ocho, which is warm and crowded, and all the men look as if they have been there since breakfast time, and will still be there at night. And Los Claveles, which is full of bullfighters who have failed to find winter jobs, and sit shivering in their thin summer suits, with a blank look of long-suffering in their eyes. The conversation is about Pedro, who has got an engagement in the Argentine, but who will surely lose as much as he makes in commission to his agent and in the expensive standard of living over there.

And there is Escribanía and Doña Conchita's and some others. In the cold days it is not a question of drinking, or even of seeking company: it is passing from brasero to brasero. A few steps, and you are chilled to the bone, your teeth chatter, your face aches with the cold—but there is another tavern, and the warmth of charcoal, of human bodies, of the wine smell, which greets you with cheerful comfort, at the swinging open of a door. Everyone is very kind, very welcoming, very pitiful to everyone else—but there is hardly any talk. 'So-and-so died yesterday.' 'There is a mass at the Angustias for So-and-so.' Such information is laconically exhanged; no one is affected. Death is busy; it may occupy itself with you tomorrow—or the next day. *Quien sabe? Es el invierno.* I wonder if it is wholly by accident that the Spanish words for winter and hell so closely approximate.

All the way up the hill, under the dripping elms, I continue to wonder. What is there, for instance, in the atmosphere of this place that induces a penitential mood; that forbids one to avail oneself of the screeling little tramway, or of the taxi-cabs on the Plaze Nueva, whose drivers are sunk into lethargy under coverings of newspapers, as though anxious to discourage possible fares?

After the quiet of the town, the noise of the water is deafening; it is like walking under cascades, our ears ring with it, it beats in and on our brains, an actual pain of sound. The rain has stopped, but one hardly notices it under the trees, that hurl down their burden of water upon the cobbles. We cannot hear our own footsteps, and the effort of ascent brings no more than a faint intimation of warmth to our limbs. We can feel the snow that we cannot see, whose melted torrents race past us down the hillsides.

On the Campo de los Martires are a few gipsies, driven by despair out of their caves on the Sacromonte, where there is no money and no food, to beg in the hotels and the Alhambra villas. Their faces are greeny-grey, like slate, the lips a livid purple; they hold out thin, frozen claws, while no sound issues from their anguished lips. The Campo is a sea of mud, the blackened myrtles make a *crêpe*-like border between the wall and the sky coloured like an old tent. We lean against the wind.

It is something, with the closing of a door, to shut out that noise of waters: not completely, for its echoes are in every crack and cranny, in every ill-fitting shutter and clacking gate.

There is nothing to do but go to bed. That is all, really. That is what one had been doing for a week. The servant fills hot bottles, and we pile our wet coats on top of the blankets, where they begin to steam as the heat comes through. The beds are uneven, of old, old flock in clotted lumps, to which one has learned, after months, to adjust one's anatomy, and the blankets are threadbare. Without our coats we should be frozen. Each bed slopes either towards, or away from, the wall, and feels, when one first gets into it, damp with the cold and the humidity of the stones themselves.

In your room you sleep, I think . . . while I lie wondering what human perversity brought me to this place, to this house of the Dead Moor: and what super-perversity keeps me in it, when three days of sea-travel, or a day and a night in train and aeroplane, will bring me all the amenities of civilization, of central heating, of hot baths, of comfortable bedding and impeccable sanitation.

With each gust of wind, a little more plaster patters from the walls, a torn *persana* shuffles on the balcony; as the early darkness falls, the noise of water mounts, until it seems as though all the streams of the Alhambra are using the dead house for a channel, and a low, continuous wailing, coming from the Vega, wraps the house in a thin winding-sheet of fear. The window-panes blacken, and in each appears the shrivelled orange of the one, unshaded electric light—too far from the bed to serve for reading—that each blast sets swinging on its cord attached to the sagging ceiling. The spiders' webs hang in each corner like the wings of bats, because they are just too high for Encarnacíon to reach with her feather broom. The brasero gives out no heat, but fills the room with its acrid stench of charcoal.

As time wears on, I reach the explanation of my presence in this cheerless room, cramped in this comfortless bed, shrinking from draughts and choking in charcoal fumes.

It is something like having a friend who, having regaled one richly in his days of prosperity, falls upon evil times. Setting aside nobler sentiments, self-respect prevents one from allowing the friendship to lapse. It is possible, even, that one may exaggerate it: may exert an assiduity in excess of one's true sentiments—which, in prosperous times, one would have been at less pains to disguise.

One lives, where this friend is concerned, in agonies of delicacy: dreading equally accusations of neglect or suspicions of patronage. One discovers a morbid punctiliousness in keeping assignations: whereas, in the old days, one would lightly have defaulted, and as lightly excused oneself at a later meeting—telephone wires, telegraph forms and even the post are summoned to assure the friend that only catastrophic events have forced one to break one's appointment. Whereas one saw him, perhaps once a month, one forms the habit of looking him up once a fortnight, or even once a week: and perhaps the meetings do not contribute much to the pleasure of either. For it is possible that this fellow owed a great part of his attraction to his affluence, and that, robbed of the wherewithal to surround himself with the necessary attributes of his personality, he is but a dull dog, and one's minds have little in common. But thus it is; and one is obliged, even at the sacrifice of personal taste, to lay balm to one's *amour propre*.

Thus it is: that, having taken from Granada the glory of her matchless Springs and Summers, the splendour of her Autumns, I find myself constrained to watch with her through her spiritual night. It is, if you like, a cementing of love; it is my first conscious attempt to draw nearer the spirit of Granada, to her cold, embittered aloofness, her everlasting pessimism, which I have felt, even in her fiesta days. Under the burden of her vines and her roses, through the song of her nightingales and the music of her guitars, I have sensed some of that which it is her pride to conceal: that Granada is a dying town, a town which has taken centuries to die, and in whose ashes fire still lingers, reluctant to depart.

Strip her of her superficial summer romanticism, and you discover a cankered loveliness that plants a spear in the heart. But in rejecting the canker, you reject the soul of Granada: you reject the mysterious source from which she draws, not only her weakness, but her strength.

CHAPTER IX

SANTA CRUZ

G RANADA, I am seriously assured by my little friend, the bomb manufacturer in the calle de Goméres, is full of Reds. I accept the fact, as I accept the tacit assurance that the neat little hand-grenades, which he arranges to set, or dry, or simmer, or whatever is the correct procedure with bombs, on his balcony, are intended to explode and do great damage to capitalist property. One of the little bombs, not much larger than a pine-cone, rolls off the balcony one day, blows a little hole in the pavement and slightly damages the façade of Messrs. Cooks Wagons-Lits. Its author is shocked, is prostrate with apologies for the misadventure. The girls in the lace-and-fan shop are chattering, cursing him like a flock of outraged parakeets across their frames of stretched net with the cobwebby pomegranates. The bomb-maker is in disgrace, is sent to coventry. I try to console him.

'You will have plenty of opportunity next week, when they open the new university buildings, to put your little bombs to their proper use!'

'*Ay*, senora! But here is what it is of truly unfortunate! It is upon that very day my friends and I have arranged a party in the country!'

Zamora comes to open the university—to the strains of the military bands, whose welcoming blasts do not, unhappily, quite synchronize; and no bombs are thrown until the evening, when once might say for the honour of the cause a little hand grenade is tossed on the Gran Vía, scaring the young girls on the *paseo*, and sending the old woman who keeps the newspaper kiosk squawking out of her temple of literature like a hen with its coop falling about its ears. And, true to the paradoxical flavour which clings to such affairs in this town of Granada, it presently transpires that the kiosk—the only property to suffer damage—is the distributing centre for Red Propaganda.

At least, there is some argument as to whether it is actually this one, or another, upon the Plaza Nueva. With its love of drama and of the ludicrous incident, Granada insists it is the Gran Vía kiosk; but the addict to proven fact is obliged to admit that it is about the Plaza Nueva kiosk that the loungers from the Cuartel district linger, and it was there that a Civil Guard who took too pressing an interest in their activities was most abominably shot in the back, on another occasion.

Granada is full of Reds. Yet the tremendous figure of Nuestra Señora de las Augustias, with the dead Christ across her knees, and the bullion-laden velvet of her robes pouring across the shoulders of her supporters, is still borne rocking through the streets, followed by sober gentlemen who carry in their black-gloved hands the candles of brown wax which, in the sunlight, bend into croquet-hoops and are most difficult to manipulate with the dignity that belongs to the gentleman of Granada, when he witnesses publicly to his faith.

The only people to show a cynical indifference to the holy spectacle are the Church officials, who, fully vestmented, nod and wink to their supporters along the route. Balconies are laden and draped with shawls and carpets in the traditional fashion; old ladies, prim girls, serious-minded men of business genuflect and cross themselves as the procession passes: as the waxen tears, melting a little, like the candles, in the sunlight, glitter on the face of the Virgin—that face like a daisy, ringed by its goffered frill of lace. Beggars stare stupefied at the tremendous crown—only a replica of that presented by the last Alfonso, but glass and gilding, twenty feet up in air, are not readily distinguished, save by the knowledgeable, from gold, rubies and sapphires.

A few louts in shirt sleeves chew gum, spit and laugh to show their independence of this parade of superstition.

'Granada,' breathes the little bomb-maker at my elbow, anxiously fingering his holy medal, 'is full of Reds.'

He points downwards at these street-corner scrapings, these hungry proselytes of a creed they are too ignorant to understand.

'In them', murmurs the visionary of Goméres, 'lies the hope of Spain.'

Meanwhile, the Hope of Granada goes on her splendid way, leaving behind her a feeling of peace and benediction that inclines every man's heart lovingly towards his neighbour.

Granada is full of Reds. Along the pavements for a few days in each month of May appear clusters of little girls, who, in the days of Catholic education, were prim, shy and modest as their elder sisters, but, under secular and political instruction, have developed a pert boldness, and who hold out their hands with the assurance of infant highwaymen, to importune the stranger.

'*Santa Cruz, Santa Cruz. Un centimo para la Cruz.*'

On the tin lids they offer are scattered a few flower petals, and, among the petals, as a decoy, a *perra gorda*. The South must infuse even its begging with this touch of grace.

Although bold, they are not impudent, and it is a hardened person who refuses his tribute to the Holy Cross. Down on the Salón, and at the tables in front of the Café de la Alameda, stout men thrust their fists into their pockets, shoddily smart young clerks and the innumerable army of *faineants* who exist from dawn to dusk on a few cups of coffee and a cigarette scrounged from their better-off friends, fling down *perra chicas* with the air that goes with the bestowal of thousands, and smile on the young beguilers. It is a mechanical gesture: so mechanical that I have seen as many pennies contributed by people wearing the badges of the workers' unions as by known pillars of the Church and Society.

When the whole of the Reyes Católicos turns the colour of the heart of a rose, and a few minutes after glimmers into a greenness of aquamarine, before fading into the starlit dark, a flight of little butterflies makes its début upon the plazas.

No Communist instruction nor the singing of the Internacional nor the indiscipline of schools can rob the little Granadina of this one night in the year, when, with the proud connivance of her parents, she blossoms into an infanta, with her bright embroidered shawl, her ankle-length frock of many flounces, her piled-up curls, bright-coloured combs and carnations pressed behind her ears. Shedding hoydenism as a chicken sheds the broken shell, an immense, traditional dignity transforms this five or six-year-old brigand of the pavements. Clinging shyly by her mother's hand, or throned on her father's shoulder, her proud and distant gaze disclaims acquaintance with you, the part-provider of her present glory, as much as with that importunate moppet who, a few short hours ago, flicked its alms-tin under your very nose.

Paul, Juana and I go down the town, to view the decorated patios; Enrique, at his own request, is included in the party, because, as he earnestly insists, Granada is full of Reds, and it would be very awkward if we had not some well-known person to protect us, in the event of any demonstration. Dubious of Enrique's qualifications as protector, we accept, nevertheless, his escort: kindly refraining from pointing out that, so far as physical defence is concerned, Paul is a good twelve inches, Juana ten inches, and I, perhaps, nine and a half inches taller than our small, fat guide, who pushes his hat at an angle, grasps his English walking-stick, which he says a tourist gave him, and does all possible to convince us that we are bent on a desperate expedition.

The moon swims over Granada; the quiet streets, linked with the white ribbon moonlight, with the silver threads of guitar music that go looping from *reja* to *reja*, is serenity itself.

Everywhere we go we are invited to enter and see the Holy Crosses. We peer through *rejas* at lighted interiors, rich and brilliant as the backgrounds to medieval canvases, at crosses made out of carnations, out of fans, out of twisted shawls. Where we enter, we deposit a *peseta* each on the tray placed to receive the offerings; the money goes to local charities, and is a trifle to pay for the charming and exotic spectacle which greets us in every house.

Prizes are offered by the town for the most richly decorated *patios*, and we argue hotly among ourselves about the respective merits of one smothered in masses of the palest carnations, and another, belonging to a bullfighter's family, where all the trophies of the ring—the rich magenta capes, the pink and green paper-trimmed banderillas, the swords and muletas, even the great head of a Miura bull, are used as accessories to the Cross itself, which is placed against a background formed by the magnificent fighting suit of a matador; and, so arguing, arrive at a street, the entrance to which is cut off by a heavy curtain, slung on a wire from side to side.

At this point Enrique justifies his presence, for we should have been too diffident to enter without his escort. All is politeness and welcome when we pass into a little cul de sac, transformed, it seems, into a dance hall.

Along each wall and on the balconies the tenants display all the riches of their households: the braseros of copper and brass, the great ewers and bowls of painted faience that have been in their families for generations. Shawls, carpets and bedspreads change the aspect of the street into that of an oriental bazaar, and remind one how close and unbreakable is the spiritual link that joins the ranges of Atlas and Nevada.

A gay little amateur band is mounted on an improvised dais; the dancers move joyously, beer is handed at the little tables set out on the pavements; an air of irresistible and innocent happiness envelops and entrains one with the gentle company.

'Granada,' mutters Enrique, feeling that he is slipping out of the picture, and seeking a means of making himself important, 'is full of Reds'—and scowls at a dancing couple who laugh back in his face.

The stars are cracklingly bright. We drink ice-cold beer. We forget, for a while, to discuss the *patios*. Someone has produced castañettas, and, in a twinkling, the sevillana is in progress, that most beautiful of all group dances, that complete expression of the soul of Andalucía, that makes the young men forget their cheap American-style suits, that lifts their arms in the air and displays all the grace of their bending torsos, as they meet their partners and retreat and weave their way from step to step—exactly as their grandparents and great-grandparents did, in an age when red was merely a bright and beautiful colour that made darker a girl's dark eyes, or defined the slenderness of a youth's swaying hips. All the night becomes incredibly beautiful, and tender, and loving. . . .

Paul and Juana are tired; have gone home to bed; and Enrique and I move silently across one of those white, broken spaces that lie in the heart of Granada: where the dust rises above one's ankles at each step and the ruins of old Moorish houses blink blind eyes at the passing of a stranger. An air of evasion, of secrecy lies on this neighbourhood; it is etiquette, one feels, not to observe too closely any figure that slips in or out of the broad, low doorways. The very cats, perched in *rejas* behind which no candle shows, ignoring our existence, fix their pale, immutable gaze upon things that were visible, perhaps, in the days of Bibirambla.

As we emerge opposite a tavern which Enrique knows too well, and I well enough: as our shadows splay out on the white dust ahead of us—there is a rush, my arm is caught, and La Fea, with whom I have a polite acquaintance, based on the friendliness of her small black puppy with my Lorenzo, begs me to come and see her Cross.

I am charmed, particularly as I have always had a curiosity about La Fea's dwelling—a high, frowning relic of Moorish pride at right angles to the tavern. To the discomposure of Enrique, I allow myself to be drawn across the threshold, where La Fea's friends greet me with gusts of French perfume, with crimson blaze of lipsticks, with hospitable head-tossings that set tremendous pendants swinging in pink ears, nested in their curls like plovers' eggs in beds of parsley.

'*Qué gloria!*' I am driven to exclaim at least a score of times, while I am taken from stage to stage of the impressive spectacle, whose apex is, of course, the Holy Cross.

There is a raised altar, approached, like that of a cathedral, by a long flight of steps, along each tread of which carnations are strewn in abundant sheaves of colour, their crushed heads giving up an overpowering perfume. Carnations, too, are scattered upon the vast manila shawl that covers the altar. Before the reredos of another fabulous shawl, the ivory Christ extends His arms along a shaft of gold and ebony, and conceals His wounded feet in a sheaf of blood-red carnations. Candles blaze to left and right of the crucifix. Tilted above the Holy Figure, in a rococo gilt frame of ecclesiastical origin, is the immense coloured oleograph of the Virgin of the Angustias, that is as much a *sine qua non* of the Granadino household as the family Bible of its British counterpart. Amid its grandiloquent surroundings, even this outrage on a sensitive taste acquires a kind of hideous splendour of its own.

I lay, in profound silence, a whole *duro*—five *pesetas*—upon the collection plate. I regret enormously that Paul and Juana are not with us, to add their assurances to mine that this is indeed the finest Cross in the town, and am making my adieux—when in comes a band of young men with guitars and a great zest for playing thereon; their greeting is vociferous, their familiarity with La Fea and her friends indubitable, and, 'in a trice', as the fairy tales have it, I am abducted by Enrique, and we are out again in the moonlit dust.

Enrique professes an immense moral disturbance, that an *inglesa* should enter the house of La Fea, even if it be no farther than the patio, and on a night of the Holy Cross, and begs me seriously not to betray him to Paul and Juana, who he considers would take a very poor view of the affair; but, pressed, he sees no more reason than I why the best Cross in Granada should not be found in a brothel— 'for, of course, the girls earn plenty of money, and can afford extravagances that are not within the reach of respectable people!'

CHAPTER X

LOS BUFONES

O<small>LD</small> Josefa, whose face looks as though it were carved from a Brazil nut, and whose left eye is blinded with cataract, makes fatalistic movements between the little box edges with a palm leaf broom. Her warped figure, draped in black that has gone olive green with age and weather, is shrivelled like a cobweb in the blasts of hate which, overnight, have burned up the house and the tavern and the little L-shaped garden and the *patio* where a tiny fountain tosses its trembling jet towards the overhanging vines; and all the Albaicin buzzes with the history of last night's happenings at the Villa Luisa.

Angustias, the half-starved, half-wit general servant, mother of four little hybrid scarecrows who sit shivering on the doorstep like a clutch of frightened sparrows, looks as though the devil were on her heels; and small wonder, for Luisa's face is like the Medusa's—a lamp beaten out of thin grey lead, with hell fire smouldering in the empty eye sockets.

This she rapidly conceals as we enter the *patio*—Lorenzo and I. Lorenzo has had a bath, a cologne friction and a bowl of milk; smugly self-satisfied, he bestows a patronizing lick on Luisa, whose greetings are divided between *el perrito* and his mistress.

'*Que tal, Luisa?*'

In a flash, she is the martyr, the victim, the tormented heroine of a thousand outrages; her eye collects her trembling audience, which, taking courage from the presence of a stranger, draws a little nearer, and prepares to play its accustomed rôle of chorus to Luisa's elegiacs. They dare

99

not do otherwise: a hint of disagreement, or of contradiction, and what vengeance will she not take on them?—this hell-cat of the calle de la Parra, this angel of the market-place,

Fascinated, as always, by the duality of Luisa's character, I listen to her version of the night's adventure. We are joined by one-eyed María la Cabrera, who, as her family is supported almost entirely by Doña Luisa, is prepared to swear her soul away in support of her benefactress's statements.

Miguel has taken a knife to her! Drunk as a pig, he has threatened her with death—and before all these witnesses. Next time I pay a visit to the Albaicín there will probably be nothing of Luisa but her mutilated body, laid out upon the bed she bought with her own money . . . and what about that for shame?—that idle sponger Miguel never having, since the day they were married—a bad shadow on that day!—contributed a *perra chica* to the upkeep of his home. Did they—she swings upon her audience—did they, or did they not, see him seize the knife and spring on her to murder her?

Of course they did: although, as subsequent inquiry brings forth, Angustias was at home, giving her children their supper, old Josefa had gone to visit her sick daughter, and María the goatherd had just stepped out for a litre of vinegar. Through stone walls and across a network of alleys they saw it: or God help them if they didn't!

Rocking backwards and forwards under the quinces, I do my best to look like a female Solomon. At all events, I do not by look or word betray that Luisa's narrative is ancient history: that earlier in the morning, while drinking my coffee, the bell of the *cancela* rang, and Rosario, who is snobbish about my Albaicín acquaintances, came down to say, with an air of disapproval, that Don Miguel is there, and wishes to see me.

'I told him it was too early to disturb the señora.'

'Ask Don Miguel to join me here, and bring another cup.'

Her stiff little back expresses her remonstrance, but, as usual, she obeys without argument. Like everyone outside the scintillating rays of Luisa's influence, she has to admit

that Don Miguel is '*buen*' *persona*', and that it is a great
pity others do not acknowledge it.

Miguel has the air of a gentle wolf, as he bows and makes
apologies for his early call. Tall, florid of complexion,
with high castellano features that are improved by the
casual attentions of the barber, his naturally mild hazel eyes
are lent a spurious fierceness by the wild growth of jet black
hair across the bridge of his nose. His costume suggests a
river picnic: zip-fastened American shirt, loose slacks of
pale grey flannel and a dark jacket slung haphazard across
his shoulders. Anyone less likely to threaten a woman with
a knife can hardly be imagined. He has some humour, much
melancholy, and a passion equal to Luisa's for being the
centre of the stage. In duplicity he is not quite her equal,
but he makes up for this with much greater artistry in his
deceptions. This is because he is better educated: less of a
materialist; more of a philosopher.

He presents to me, with inimitable grace, a posy hastily
assembled of flowers from my own garden: a little golden
rose, a sprig of plumbago, a slip of myrtle. He sits down, but
is nervous and restless, and accepts with relief my offer of a
little cognac in substitution for the cup of coffee.

Luisa is a madwoman. Madre mia, she is a monster. How
can a man be expected to exist with a monster? Yet who will
believe it—so kind, so generous is she, to all save her
husband!

'Well, Miguel, why don't you get a divorce? You know it
is not so difficult as it was before the Republic.'

'Señorita Margarita. I would give all I possess to be
divorced from Luisa. She is like a sickness, she devours me
like a vulture. What is the remedy? It is she who will not
divorce, because, according to the civil law, divorce means
an equal division of our property. What would I not give to
take my share and never set eyes on her again!—to escape
from her claws and make myself a new life, in Mexico,
perhaps, or the Argentine! But the señorita knows what she
is: she is avaricious beyond description. She would stand
like the Stone Commander and watch me perish in the
gutter, before she would part with a *perra chica*.'

'*Ay, ay*, Miguel. It is very sad about you and Luisa. You must have loved her very much when you married her.'

As though he feels the change in its colour, he lifts his hand and passes it across his suddenly livid face.

'Have I never told the señorita?—I had been away, studying the law, and I came back on a Sunday when there was a bullfight. Like all young men, I was mad about the bulls, and I went to look for my friend who was Luisa's brother, and who lived with her and the old grandmother in a house near the Puerta Real. I had not seen Luisa since she was a little girl.

'*Pues* . . . the door was opened to me by the divinest creature I ever saw. Later on, I heard they called her the Queen of the Puerta Real. Señorita Margarita, I did not go to see the bulls.'

'*Qué simpatico?*'—I replenish Miguel's glass.

'So we became lovers. I cared no longer for anything else; my law studies were abandoned. *Quê salero, quê salero tenía mi mujer!*'

It is a few moments before he can continue.

'When the time came that it was not enough for us to be together for a few hours each night, I hired a horse and we rode into the mountains, Luisa behind me, on a blanket, like a gipsy. We found an inn to sleep, with the smallest bed in the world: but it was not too small for us. Sometimes, señorita, looking at that great silver bed Luisa has bought, which she hates sharing with me, I am tempted to remind her of nights when a plank in a mountain inn was wide enough for such lovers as we were.'

'. . . Miguel. Are you sure you hate her?'

'Hate her?—If it were not for the scandal, I should laugh with joy if I were today to follow her coffin up the Alhambra hill!'

'*Callate*—that's a dangerous thing to say, in a place where there are so many bad tongues.'

'Señorita Margarita.' Miguel looks pained and crosses his fingers like a gipsy. 'She had denied me food all day. I was ravenous. I was cutting myself a piece of bread. I had not even a few pence to buy a glass of cognac, and she accused me of being drunk. I—who am not even permitted to take a *copita* in my own tavern! I had the knife in my hand; she threw herself towards it . . .

'I am here to inform the señorita that it is my unalterable intention to go this day before the magistrates, to find out if there is no way in which an honest man can be delivered from the torments of hell and a wicked wife!'

'Well, Miguel, I think it is a good idea. If you are sure there is no hope of making it up with Luisa.'

He shakes his head slowly, fingering the bristle about his long, wolf-like chin.

'I have reached my conclusions, and I now come to beg a great favour of the señorita.'

'It is already granted,' I say politely.

'The señorita can witness to my character,' pleads Miguel earnestly. 'I am not like Luisa: I cannot bribe a score of people to tell lies on my behalf. It is necessary that there should be someone of good standing, to prove that I am a misjudged character: and who can make so fortunate an impression as the señorita, who is known to all, who is without prejudice, and who can have no motive, save that of honour, for supporting a defenceless man?'

'I depend on you,' says Luisa passionately, 'to act as my witness. These poor creatures!'—she waves a hand of contemptuous pity at the circle of her satellites—'who will pay attention to these? They are so ignorant, they will lose courage when they are asked questions. What an impression it will make when I say to the magistrate, "Señor, I do not ask Your Honour to believe me, a poor tavernkeeper of the Albaicin; but this señora—noble, distinguished, upright as all the English are!—you will attend to her when she assures you that I am dying by inches of my life with the greatest wretch in Granada, a villain beside whom Judas Iscariot was innocent as a little lamb—"'

'Quite, quite.' I hastily stem the torrent of Luisa's eloquence. 'Of course, it makes no difference that I have never been present at any of the scenes you describe, between you and Miguel?'

'What difference can it make?' coos Luisa, in her voice of a deep-throated dove. 'The señora knows I would never lie to her; is she not my friend, my protectress? Do I not lay my whole trust in her, as in the tablets of stone?'

The Plaza Nueva burns white with midday sun, and we pass with relief into the stone-coolness of the Ayuntamiento, furling our fans, loosening the *velos* that hang limp with the heat of our hair.

Behind us troops Luisa's inseparable retinue: old Josefa, the fool Angustias, one-eyed María, María's horrible small boy, Antonio, and Paco, the soft-voiced, gentle-eyed gipsy boy who waits on the customers at night. Luisa, in her best black silk, walks at the head of her procession like a queen, spilling her smiles right and left with reckless abandon, 'enchanted' to meet this person and 'elated' to meet that: as though the occasion were wholly a social one, as though nothing were further from her mind than laying a charge of attempted murder against her husband.

At this hour of the morning, the courts are crowded—by suitors who have a pleasant air of having come prepared to spend the day, the week, the month, if necessary. Small domestic parties, cosily settled on the benches, offer the hospitality of their baskets to newcomers, who decline with the classic formula, 'Many thanks; good appetite to you.'

A group of witnesses from the country districts—their broad straw hats shading faces of almost negroid blackness, and their breeches of oyster-coloured corduroy tinged with the rose pink of the earth in which they labour—are solemnly and politely accepting bribes from a business-like person in a black Cordobés. The magistrates' clerks, smoking *canarios* and exchanging comments on the few pretty girls who lean, eyelids heavy with boredom, against the stone pillars, break off to eye our little cortège with interest. An extraordinary number of dogs wanders through and around the place, amusing the spectators with their amatory gambols, and exciting Lorenzo, whose plump body, like a small black satin bolster, stiffens in my arms, as he emits futile growls of scorn for the scabrous multitude.

There is a slightly awkward moment, when we come face to face with Miguel, skulking, it must be admitted furtively, behind a pillar: but so thoroughly has the dramatic occasion mounted to Luisa's head, so charmed is she by the publicity which accrues to her through the presence of '*la inglesa*', that she greets him as a bosom friend. Miguel and I exchange winks; I do my best to make mine reassuring, for I have—let's face it—a soft spot for Miguel, and am fully prepared, having served Luisa's purpose, to bear witness on his behalf.

Miguel disappears—I think for a glass of *aguardiente*—and Luisa and I and the draggletails are ushered into one of the courts: a dim place like an immense well, with a stone bench running entirely round the walls, and, at the farther end, a dais, on which, behind a table littered with papers, sits the magistrate, a clerk, and somebody's solicitor.

The bench gives at first the impression of being draped with cobwebs, but, as one's eyes accustom themselves to the gloom, these resolve themselves into the suitors, who seem to have been there since the beginning of time: to have grown old and colourless and fleshless in waiting for the slow progress of some dim justice which they have not the wit properly to invoke. The magistrate pays no attention to them whatever, excepting when the chatter reaches too piercing a crescendo, when a clerk bellows 'Silence!', in a voice usually kept for the quelling of rebellious dogs.

We seat ourselves meekly—the draggletails at a respectful distance from their mistress, Antonio lolling against her knee, and Lorenzo on mine. I can see in Luisa's eye the consideration of whether it might be possible to pass off Antonio as her ill-used child, and thus working up the drama of her own appearance. The little wretch has already been primed with a full eye-witness account of the drama of the knife, and I have warned Luisa that if she calls Antonio as a witness I shall throw in my hand. She whispers excitedly: 'There is good fortune—I feel it! You always bring it to me—you are our good angel! And you will see: because of your presence we shall have immediate attention.'

She seems to be correct in her surmise. A breathless silence has fallen, and every eye is on our little group. Presently a clerk comes down, and, addressing me, asks very politely if there is any business to which he can attend for me. I wave him on to Luisa, who rises, begins a smothered flood of explanation, and is abruptly checked. But the clerk, who has received, apparently, some mysterious communication from the magistrate, again bows to me, and says, 'The señoras are invited to take their places at the table.'

Luisa is ready to explode with gratification. With an imperious gesture to her retinue, with a glance towards the onlookers, which says, more plainly than any words, 'You see what a person of importance I am!', she swims towards the dais, waving her fan with the languor of a Court beauty. She shows no signs of mortification when the magistrate brushes her aside, leaps from his chair, insists upon my taking the seat of honour, and beams with as much pleasure as if we were meeting at a garden party.

He repeats my name, when Luisa introduces us, as though it were a rhapsody: 'La señorita Margarita Es-tín!' He makes many bows, pays, rapidly, many compliments. He then turns with a brusque air to Luisa—who is bursting with her delayed narrative—nodding sharply to her, while he smiles at me. I begin to find this faintly embarrassing, and turn my attention to Lorenzo, who, being bored, starts to be tiresome.

The magistrate gently pulls Lorenzo's insignificant tail.

Lorenzo, inebriated by so much attention, makes frantic efforts to climb on the table; I call him a granuja, which so delights the magistrate that he cuts short one of Luisa's finest periods to pick up the puppy and place him on his blotting pad. At this point Luisa, catching her breath, flashing her white teeth, is evidently thinking out a very unpleasant reprisal for Lorenzo, when—

'And what,' says the magistrate, encouraging Lorenzo to growl at a ruler, 'is the Señorita Margarita Es-tín's view on this question?'

I promptly say that I have no views, not having been present at the knife episode, but that my acquaintance with the belligerent pair leads me to think that it is an unfortunate situation for both, and would better be resolved by the law—during which discourse Lorenzo gambols, bites the corners of title deeds, snarls at a lighted cigarette still smouldering in an ash-tray, and, while Luisa, rightly feeling that she is being edged out of the picture, cries aloud of insult, outrage and murder—makes water on the magistrate's blotting pad.

A yell goes up from the audience—now withdrawn from the benches, and clustered as closely as discipline permits about the dais. Luisa, checked in her flights of fancy, gapes, allows her jaw to drop, and lets out a whoop of laughter behind her fan. The magistrate roars, congratulates me on the 'saltiness' (an Andalucían phrase which is actually untranslatable) of my little dog: wrings my hand, and implores me to dine with him—with his mother as *dueña*. Lorenzo's vulgar behaviour has completed the collapse of his official personality.

He waives aside Luisa's plea: that will do for another day—for tomorrow—for next week—if the parties have not changed their minds by then.

Burdened with guilt, I look towards Luisa for pardon—to find the unaccountable woman beaming, glittering with satisfaction. My glance travels past her, to find Miguel, also on the broad grin across the shoulder of Angustias; and, mentally cursing these inconsequent Granadinos, I make my farewells.

Once more our procession crosses the *patio*, distinguished this time by an indecent air of *romería*, of picnic party gaiety. Even the witless Angustias smiles toothlessly, old Josefa chuckles like a nightjar, and one-eyed María's voice rises in the screech of an eagle, to proclaim to all and sundry the terrific success we have made.

'But, Luisa! We have wasted time; you have gained nothing whatever!'

'Gained nothing?—Is it nothing that we are upon the most friendly terms with Don Rafael himself?—and a hundred people at least there to see it? The news will be all over Granada by now. I have nothing to do in future but walk into the Town Hall, to get all the attention I want, as though I were the Queen of Spain!'

Miguel chimes in:

'Enough has been done to show that we are people of consequence; Luisa has been asked to sit at the table—they are bound to do the same for me. Some other time—when it is convenient—I will go and see Don Rafael.'

The taxi arrives, and we enter it with the gaiety of a bridal party. Miguel and Luisa sit side by side, with their backs to the driver, virtually ignoring my existence, while they engage in the most amicable of discussions on tavern politics. One would say a model Albaicin couple, linked by the most powerful of interests, their mutual livelihood.

'*Hombre!*' coos Luisa.

'*Mujer!*' booms Miguel, pushing a loose hairpin back into Luisa's coil . . .

What indeed is a divorce, or a knifing, beside the excitement and distinction of having made an appearance in the courts: being treated with preference before an envious public: and leaving on terms of what practically amounts to intimacy with the magistrate?

Miguel is as pleased as though it had been he who received the compliment, and the disgraceful hero of the morning's burlesque sleeps like an angel across my knee. I am a little thoughtful. Is it possible I have been, for once, a victim of the Granadino sense of humour?

CHAPTER XI

TERTULIA

'You must meet', says Frasquito, 'my great friend, Don Santiago Carbonnel.' (It is not his real name, but that does not matter; it is a name already known to me, which carries weight in the province, and which attaches to a fine vine-growing estate down on the Vega.)

It appears Don Santiago has invited us to supper, and, in the usual fashion, a car arrives, between ten and eleven, and we set forth.

There is still stupendous heat, and I have a mild attack of fever. I am beginning to appreciate fever—its part in the enchantment of the emotional tempo of whatever one happens to be doing. When the temperature skids up over the hundred mark, there is a corresponding glitter in all that one feels, says and does, and, if the aftermath is a little less pleasing, there is always the soothing recollection (or illusion) of past brilliance to sustain one through present gloom.

There is also a blasting moonlight, which makes black pits of the excavations in the road—little better than a cart track—along which no English chauffeur would venture his vehicle. Careless of his back axle, Pedro plunges on, encouraged by our shouts of congratulation each time we evade disaster; Pedro shouts back, because he is a great driver, and his is a great car, and because he is going to Don Santiago's, where wine flows like water from Avellano springs: but mainly because he is driving Don Frasquito, whose nocturnal exploits have made him the hero of all the Granadino chauffeurs.

We have with us Frasquito's guitarrista, the gentle-mannered, exquisitely polite Miguel. His pale, innocent, monk-like face is slightly shadowed with anxiety for his precious instrument, as we are flung wildly from side to side. Miguel is giving me lessons on the guitar. Each evening, about sunset he arrives, meek, diffident to the point of evaporation, and we work for an hour. His patience is inexhaustible, his devotion to his task a thing of religion, above and beyond all recognition of personalities, of human relationships. If the work goes well, he will presently play to me. There is dusk on the terrace, and in the lower gardens falls silence, as the chords of Falla and Albeñiz drop through the meshes of wistaria. Alas, that Falla himself should have been driven away by the roaring of radio on the Alhambra hill!

We arrive at high iron gates, set between towering pillars of brickwork, and are suddenly in the midst of the vineyards. Under a lighted cloister, whose pillars support the upper storey of the long, pale house, Don Santiago receives us in a patriarchal group which includes the two mothers—sisters—of his five splendid sons.

Don Santiago is short and plump, a true 'son of the vine stock': of an old Andalucían family which, after falling on evil days, has been suddenly restored to something of its former prosperity by the discovery of lead mines on some hitherto disregarded property. Don Santiago has put all his share of the family patrimony into his vineyards, and in distinction from most of the landowners in this part of Spain, is a violent adherent of the Government party.

No shadow of politics, however, blurs the warmth and grace of his greeting, the lofty and unembarrassed courtesy with which we are presented to '*mi mujer*', whom I take to be the original wife, and '*su hermana*', a serene handsomeness who holds the youngest son, a boy of eleven or twelve, by the hand. Nor, by any means, does this complete the introductions, for a smiling young woman in white, with a plump baby in her arms, offers her hand with a friendly dignity which establishes her right to be included in the family circle, and Frasquito seizes an early opportunity of informing me that the infant is the latest addition to the Carbonnel family, and its mother, Asunción, the last upon whom the patriarch's favours have fallen.

Here, indeed, we come upon the Moorish root! Nothing appears gross, nothing unseemly in this distribution of favour. No signs of preference appear, on Don Santiago's part; of jealousy, on the part of the wives. A more serene household it is impossible to picture, held together by devotion to its head. An enviable man, Don Santiago!— listened to respectfully, and unquestioningly obeyed, by his women folk, in whose peaceful acquiescence nothing at all is reminiscent of the harem. Their mutual affection and friendliness is demonstrated in a score of trivial ways throughout the evening: each is prompt to support, to encourage the others, a current of sympathy links all their quiet actions, their glances, their few words. One may say that the polygamous ideal is admirably exemplified by this happy family, out on the Andalucían plain.

I am a spectacle to these three women: the strange spectacle of a woman, not obviously unattractive, yet unmarried (this is established within the first five minutes, in a quick aside to Frasquito), strangely free to go gadding about to foreign countries, yet apparently virtuous; holding my own in conversation with the men, yet, evidently, not resented. I baffle them: they give me up.

The two sisters—big, full-bosomed countrywomen, in grave dresses of black silk—sit down one on either side of me; the white-gowned young Asunción with her baby directly in front; and fix me with such sweet, smiling, unwinking stares of pure interest that it is impossible to feel embarrassed or offended. One of them feels, shyly, the material of my black chiffon gown.

'Qué bonita! Qué graciosa!'

'Muy cara, muy cara', says the other, tenderly reproachful, and both smilingly shake their heads. I am extravagant, indiscreet in my expenditure upon my person. My slippers come in for the same awed scrutiny. The fan slides from my lap, and all three make a swift, simultaneous movement to pick it up.

They have no general conversation, apparently no ideas on which to found it; sweetness of disposition and unbounded curiosity take the place, in them, of social graces, and, with the best will in the world, the conversation sags. If I could have talked of household matters—of babies, and cooking, and fruit preserving—I am sure I should have had them chattering like magpies; but my ignorance of their topics is no less than their ignorance of mine.

Their eyes become blank with a purely mechanical attention the moment we diverge from dress materials, or the age and probable origin of my manila shawl. Descriptions of foreign scenes, of foreign habits go beyond their understanding; they sigh and smile angelically at one another. The children, the household, the vines are all reality, all actuality, so far as they are concerned; the rest is a fairy-tale for the little ones. A fleeting envy for these quiet lives, girdled by the mountains, ruled by the seasons, crosses my mind.

Now Don Santiago insists upon displaying the vineyard plant to his visitors. The wives meekly accept their dismissal, and go to prepare supper, while we wander away in the moonlight, to inspect the modern irrigation system and the machinery which has replaced the old wooden presses, where the labourers trampled the grapes under their bare feet. I express regret for the passing of the old order, and, somewhat to my surprise, Don Santiago agrees with me, on aesthetic, although not on economic grounds.

'You must come to our gathering, señora; you will see that we still keep up the old customs—for the people's sake; it is good for them to feel the grape juice spurting between their toes, and to sing the old songs of the grape harvest. We are getting too far away from the soil, and it is not good—either for the wine or for us.'

This develops into an argument—purely abstract and theoretical, as such arguments are apt to be—that fruit and grain are both dishonoured by contact with metal: that stone and wood only should be employed for the separation of the grain from the wheat, the liberation of its juices from the grape; which carries us into the deep caves, filled with immense terracotta vats, where the juice is fermenting. We are shown the numbered racks of vintages, invited to taste, presented with bottles.

When we return, they are waiting for us—the Three Graces, two black, one white; and the boys also are standing around, shyly graceful, in the shadows of the great palms, under which has appeared a table dappled with moonlight, and the vast terracotta jar which means that a *sangria* is to be prepared. The *sangria*, as usual, is Frasquito's business, and he brings a hieratic ceremony to the blending of the wine with the peaches, the peaches with the cinnamon. We have brought the ice out with us from Granada, in a sack under the seat of the car.

Hardly has the first glass gone round, when Miguel el Santo has plucked from his guitar a phrase of Albeñiz, in compliment to Don Santiago's *afición* for the modern composers. The notes of the guitar act astringely upon the temperaments of the listeners—all soft and relaxed with moonlight, with the ghostly sheaves of the arum lilies and with the surrounding kilometros of sleeping vineyard: and have drawn a soft, indistinct multitude of house servants and vineyard labourers into the deep shadow at the end of the garden. The sudden, rattling bravura of a cadenza shakes the palm leaves; hand on diaphragm, eyes closed, Frasquito has reached his moment of inspiration, and a sigh of ecstasy that is almost a groan goes up from the company, as though each had some personal share in the act that liberates that inimitable voice. . . .

In an hour's time the air has grown too fresh for outdoor singing; Frasquito stops, apologizes, makes excuses for the tiresome little break that ruined the last cadenza. The wives, sweet and lovely as attendant Demeters, fold up my shawl and present me with a rose, which the youngest pins in my hair; then, taking my hands, lead me into the house, where a lavish meal awaits us.

The room is cruelly lighted. Don Santiago is justifiably proud of his electric plant; yet four lights might be held to be sufficient for any normal-sized room, and in this one, which is small, there are at least a dozen, their glare increased by the white walls, and by the chromium glitter of hideous modern fitments. Apart from this, it is a charming room—the unglazed *rejas* draped with beautiful old Alpujarra curtains in stripes of orange, crimson, black and thin, glittering threads of gold; with thick Alpujarran rugs on the floor of black and white tiles; with a few handsome braseros on the walls, and a superb table of waxed olive wood, flanked with benches that match it.

We eat excessively—of olives, a magnificent *paella* and various kinds of sausages, washed down with draughts of Don Santiago's wines, and the conversation becomes very gay and general. Don Santiago and the eldest boy speak fluent French, and insist upon doing so with me, somewhat to my embarrassment, for French pronounced in the Andaluz fashion is not easy to understand. And there is more singing and more wine.

Presently I go with the Demeters to see the younger children in bed. There they lie, each in his own room—it is an enormous house—each like a small, dark, recumbent angel, with the electric light blazing full on his unconscious face. When I protest, the Demeters shake their heads. 'The señora does not understand: our children love the light.' Light is evidently a mania here, for even in the unoccupied bathrooms and lavatories—proudly displayed as proof of the sophistication of their scheme of living—two or three bulbs are blazing at full power. (When, later, I comment on this unusual extravagance to Frasquito, he does not seem to care for the implication that his countrymen, on the whole, are 'economical'. 'I have a friend in Madrid', he declares, 'who went to call on a lady, and kept the carriage waiting three days, at seven pesetas an hour!')

The moon is slipping down the sky, and it is time for departure. As Frasquito opens the door of the car, a wave of perfume sweeps out; the boys and their mothers have filled it with sweet herbs, with branches of lavender, rosemary, bay and thyme, and along the broad seat are strewn moon-white freesia and a couching of small, soft carnations, whose colour is drained away by the silver light.

The three women stand, smiling a little shyly, their arms round each other's waists; one feels that their lovely act comes from the depths of their happiness and content, one is brushed by the small wings of their pity—for having to leave idyllic bliss and return to the restless life of cities. Don Santiago rings our hands, presses me to come on a long visit, and as the car moves slowly away, the boys run by its side to open the gates. Their beautiful, smiling faces, their long limbs of young Adonises, are our last glimpse of this little earthly paradise.

CHAPTER XII

THE BULLS

(1)

MORNING

THE excitement of the bullfight begins at the moment one wakes up, to leap out of bed and anxiously scan the horizon for assurance that it is going to be 'a good day for the bulls'. There must be sun, but not too much sun, which makes confusion between a man and his shadow, and which may blind the matador at some crucial moment and cheat him of triumph; but there must be very great heat, and so much the better if there is thunder in the air.

On the afternoon when the young Atarfeño was killed in Granada, under the eyes of his family, his wife and his mistress—what an afternoon that was to have been, for he was due the next week to take the *alternativa* in Madrid, and as a compliment to his own town, he had engaged to kill six bulls—the sky pressed down upon and clung to the earth; one's lungs laboured. The sky was the colour of unpolished pewter, with a red-hot rim round the horizon. Such a day turns good, straight-fighting bulls into devils. It was a great day for the watersellers in the ring.

Wind is a calamity, for it forces the *toreros* to work with wet capes, which adds greatly to their weight and to some extent spoils the movements, while adding to the danger of the men.

But supposing it is a good, hard morning, with a solidly cloudless sky; that the leaves of the trees hang as though each were tipped with a plummet of lead; that one finds oneself having continual resource to the *pipote* that contains one's precious store of Avellano water—then one may be fairly confident of seeing something worth while, of a moment or two that will redeem the dullness even of a mediocre performance. (For bullfighters, like actors, are excessively temperamental; because you have paid sixty pesetas to see Belmonte, it does not mean that you are bound to see a masterpiece, any more than by paying ten to see those two little boys from Malaga you are likely to be disgusted. And a bull from the famous Miura ranches may, on occasion, be as disappointing as one of the *bichos* unloaded on an insignificant *novillada*. But this is part of the splendid chanciness of following the bulls.)

If you are so fortunate as to live in the town where the fight is to take place, you will surely, at some early hour of the morning, go down to see the bulls; the real enthusiasts will be there to receive them when they are brought in from the country in the heavy wooden vans which are run into the ring, and from which, as each bull is set loose by the man who stands on the roof, and jerks up the wooden shutter, it is collected by the steers, and conducted, not without some fuss and perhaps a mishap or two, into the corrales.

But if the fight is at a distance, very shortly after breakfast the car is at the door, and you start off, fifty, a hundred, two hundred or more kilometros—according to the degree of your enthusiasm—for a ride part of whose thrill is provided by the excitement of the driver. And as each kilometro of red earth slips by, with the crazy patch-work of the olivares, the verdigris-green *rejas* of each little mountain village crusted like fish-scales on the sheer rock face, and as you begin to fall in with others going the same way—so your heart beats quicken, you fall silent with emotion, for you are on your way to a rendezvous with death.

(II)

CAPEA

When we mount to the balcony of the town hall, which the *alcalde* has politely put at our disposal, we have an unrivalled view, not only of the 'ring', but of the surrounding landscape. The mountains, flushed to a garnet-purple by the light of the lowering sun, encircle us; their peaks dart up, like the summits of pine trees, towards the blazing sky. Beyond the walls of the tiny town, there is nothing but nature, at her wildest and most primitive: a world known only to the eagle and the mountain goat.

But in this tiny rift of the rocks, snatched from the wild by human creatures in search of dwelling, *feria* is in progress: the streets are lined with market booths, loaded with gaudy fairings, with bright pink sweetmeats and saffron-coloured cakes, with children's coloured toys and with butcher's meat—a luxury to the inhabitants, whose food, for many days of the year, consists of nothing better than boiled grass. Behind the booths are the big wooden palisades, that the men and boys have been roping together to enclose the square for the great event of the day—the *capea:* an event supposedly illegal, but, since the *alcalde* and the priest—the great powers of the town—are both ardent *aficionados*, the trivialities of law are evaded, and the Guardia Civil, the supposed enforcers of law, is enlisted to keep order in the 'ring' itself.

At the end of the square is the garage which houses the bull, who, like an old fashioned-actor, works up public excitement by occasionally charging the extraordinarily flimsy-looking door. But there is no danger. He is far too good an actor to make a premature appearance.

The 'ring' itself is a dusty space, carved into pits by wind and weather; it is bad luck for the bullfighter who happens to stumble on one of these while citing the bull. A few gipsies are strolling about, with red rags rolled up under their arms, and these appear to take the pits very much for granted; one of them, becoming aware of an audience, shakes out his bundle and executes a passable *mariposa*—the favourite trick of Lalanda—to a burst of ironic applause. It is one thing to do the *mariposa* in an empty ring, another to execute it under the nose of one of those wily village bulls, with every trick of the fight at his horn-tips. A self-important youth, with a bunch of banderillas under his armpit, takes it upon himself, for no visible reason, to order the gipsies out of the 'ring'; they go meekly, with backward glances that memorize every foot of that treacherous surface.

The crowded balconies are aflame with strings of pimento, whose scarlet clusters make a thick drapery upon the white façades. All the trees overhanging the square are laden with men and youths who, to make sure of their places, have been there since breakfast time, and exchange impolite backchat with the multitudes seething behind the palisades.

The town band now breaks into a thundering *paso doble*, and the *paseo* makes its appearance. Only those who have seen the *corrida* can appreciate the emotion of this moment— when each ragged form is clothed in imagination with the magnificent caparison of the matador. As the little procession comes up the centre of the square, a few people laugh, but I, for one, am touched to the heart by these Poor Knights of the ring, by their shabby clothing, by their desperate courage. Several have bare feet, one has not even a shirt to cover his staring ribs, his pitifully inadequate muscles. His neighbour, by contrast, has begged, or borrowed, a very old fighting suit, which is at least four sizes too big for him: but he thinks less of this dangerous handicap than of the glory of wearing it. There are a couple of old capes, but most of them carry, most correctly folded across their arms, nothing but the faded red rag. No *novillero*, bearing his first cape, could carry it more proudly.

Across the white dust they come, following their long shadows, meticulously in step, right arms swinging; and you can see in their fathomless eyes that it is not Guajasierra, but Sevilla, or Talavera, or Madrid, for each one. One has walked thirty kilometros, and has a thorn in his foot, but nothing short of amputation would prevent his taking part in the ceremony which has filled his thoughts for the past four months.

With great gravity and dignity they salute the balconies, from which a few coins are thrown, for encouragement. The Civil Guard makes a last sally, clears the 'ring' of all but the performers, who quietly take up their places close to the palisades, and, with a great deal of noise and 'theatre', the bull is let out.

At the *capea*, the bull is the principal actor. You may go to the *corrida* to see a great matador, or to the *novillada* to see a promising novice; but you go to the *capea* to see the bull, and nothing, after the *paseo*, compares in emotion with this moment when the bull comes out.

He comes out slowly—with immense swagger, like a star certain of his audience: a broad, rusty beast with all his weight in front, and light as a greyhound behind; with a knowing eye and horns like hat-racks. The tip of each horn is splintered like a wire bottle-brush. You see one or two look hurriedly at those horns, and hurriedly away; the youngest gipsy turns green and is quietly sick against the palisade. He does not want to die before he is a matador, and the merest scratch from that bundle of infected horn is enough to put the pennies on your eyes—at any rate in Guajasierra, to which the word antiseptic has not yet penetrated from civilized regions. The first man goes out . . .

For the first few minutes the bull is giving nothing away. He sniffs thoughtfully at the dust, lifts his *morillo*—as though to see whether it is in working order—and thoughtfully lets it down again. Then he takes a trot round the palisades, which he now and again clips with his horn—just to clear off the too-impudent youths who are dangling their legs from the top; stands still, and shivers off the flies.

It is very humiliating for the boy who, getting whiter and whiter, stamps his foot, flaps his cape and cries '*Huy, Toro!*' in a high, trembling voice of adolescence. The audience laughs unkindly and throws a few harmless missiles. The boy moves desperately, a foot or two nearer, and the bull stares coldly. Disgusted and ashamed, the boy turns on his heel and slouches towards the palisade, beckoning one of the others to come out.

The bull chooses this moment for a little run, and as, warned by the yell, the boy whips round, stands still and sneers. Everyone roars with laughter, and the boy returns angrily to his efforts. Two or three others join him, and the bull makes a few short runs, a jab or two towards the capes, then, suddenly, having thoroughly 'drawn' his opponents, reveals himself—with a rush like an express train from corner to corner, his left horn furrowing the earth: ending in a right angle turn that draws a roar from the entire audience. A few seconds later he repeats this incredible man œuvre—this time to the right. In a *corrida* you would find nothing like it: because *corrida* bulls are fighting for the first and only time in their lives, and have only their breed and their instinct to guide them. This wiseacre has learned his business in a dozen or more *capeas;* he has learned, not only how to trick his opponents, but how to manage his vast weight. Where a *corrida* bull would slide to his knees, or trip himself at the turn, he can tack and veer like a yacht in a changing wind. Right or left are the same to him—at all events until they have placed the banderillas—a trick he hates, and which always makes him lose his temper. But through the *suerte* of the cape he remains cool, *rusé*, and enjoys every moment of pitting his wits against those of the youths who, puzzled, scared to death, but not daring to show their fright before the public, forget such shreds of art as they have ever possessed, and draw hoots of scorn and ribaldry by their horrid travesties of movements that are known—at least in theory—to the youngest onlooker: who snatch and flap their capes in their shuddering attempts to execute *veronicas* that are never completed: between whose dithering calves, as one of our neighbours contemptuously observes, you could drive a coach and four.

But it is not the fighters who matter, yet, but the bull, which knows, or seems to know, instinctively which of his opponents is worth his steel. Gradually, neatly, see him eliminate the others, judging to a nicety how much effort it takes to drive them to the palisades, which they scale with the alacrity of monkeys.

It is the bull who chooses the three-cornered fight which now develops between himself, a tall, stubborn country youth, who has little but his courage to recommend him to the spectators, and the little gipsy who, having got rid of his fear with the contents of his stomach, is now passing visibly into that state of hypnosis which is the state of the true bullfighter: when nothing exists but himself and the bull, and nothing matters but that he shall show himself better than the bull.

To everyone's surprise, he suddenly, without preparation, draws the bull into a *paso de pecho* which takes it no less by surprise than the audience, whose shouts of appreciation come ringing back from the rock face, while the bull's head and feet come down, and it stands, obviously thinking the matter over; for here is someone who has made it do something it had not intended to do at all, and it is divided between good-humoured acquiescence and a touchy annoyance at being caught unprepared.

The big fellow, angry at the gipsy's triumph, goes foolishly in, and comes out four inches ahead of the horns that crash the palisade as he tops it. And now occurs one of those incidents which form sometimes the comedy, sometimes the irritation of the *capea*. Two braggarts leap into the 'ring', spoiling the *faena* the gipsy is preparing, and the bull gets his first chance.

With one twist of his big head he neatly scoops the shorter of the newcomers up on the horn. The fellow goes up, arms and legs spread-eagled, a ludicrous expression of fright and surprise on his face, and the bull rides him along the palisade. This is what the audience has been waiting for; it rocks with delight.

Two of the unlucky youth's friends, leaning over the *barrera*, pluck him off the horn on which he is impaled, and his howl of agony takes the bull so much by surprise that it stands mildly, looking upward, with one crimson and one natural-coloured horn adding to its grotesque appearance. Several of the nearby spectators address the bull affectionately by name, and good deal of crude witticism, dealing with its anatomy, blows about its ears, as it trots back into the middle of the ring.

. . . It is nearly an hour later. A professional banderillero goes in to plant the darts which the utmost efforts of the amateurs have failed to lodge in those wily shoulders. By now the excitement is frenzied, the bull is angry, the audience is clamouring for more sensation, and the wretched bullfighters are green with exhaustion, despair and humilia-tion. Two have received the *cornada*—one a mere scratch, the other a deep belly-wound which is likely to prove fatal.

With the help of the gipsy—now desperately brave—Luis Moreno of Granada plants a capital pair, and fails with his second, only getting one home, and that in a bad position, behind the *morillo*. The bull looks like an infuriated pin-cushion, and is ready to kill at sight.

The sun is plunging behind the mountains, the sky reeks of blood, and the boy who got the first *cornada* is dead.

Guajasierra says it has been a good *capea*. While the bull trots out, with the be-ribboned darts clacking behind its head, the crowd flings itself over the palisades, seethes towards the taverns; young men boast about the things they would have done if they had been in the 'ring', and older men about what they did twenty years ago, with bulls 'the size of cathedrals', and quicker than express trains. Everyone suffers from a rush of valour to the head, and a few youths profit by the general enthusiasm to sell the still reeking *banderillas* which have been deftly plucked from the bull's back, and are bought by *aficionados* as souvenirs of the occasion.

While Guajasierra gathers itself for the orgy that ends the day, the fighters, rolling their bundles under their arms, slip quietly and humbly away, to hide their humiliation of knowing that they have played but a sorry part in the long-looked-for event, to indulge in a wistfulness of 'might-have-been', and to pray for an early opportunity of retrieving their damaged reputations in some town far enough away from Guajasierra to have caught no echoes of the day's disgrace.

(III)

CORRIDA

We have seats on the *barrera*—that is to say, right in the front row, on the level of the ring; and Belmonte's sword-carrier—an elderly, respectable person in a good grey suit and a light grey fédora—has brought the basket of equipment—the swords, capes and muletas—and placed them right at our feet. Every time he comes from the ring, Belmonte's raised face, his sightless eyes—sightless because all of their vision is directed inward and backward to the scene of his struggle—will be turned towards us.

As a figure, it is not impressive, for the head is too large, the legs are too short for the body; there is none of that flexibility from the hip which one seeks in a matador; and it is this very inflexibility, they say, which gives Belmonte his stone-cold, immaculate art. Because he cannot move fast, he has to stand still; he has to depend on the wrists that swing the cape round him so closely that the bull's shoulder leaves a smear of blood on his clothes: on the psychological control that, at the end of a *faena*, when the bull is fixed, enables him to place his hand on its brow with a calmness that has almost the effect of a benediction.

Apart from the bullring at Sevilla, the Antequera ring is my favourite of all the rings I have visited in Spain. One of the few remaining old wooden bullrings, it lends itself in a peculiar fashion to the occult struggle which takes place, in a greater or less degree, between the *torero* and the bull he is handling. There are two bullfighters who, above all, make me conscious of this occult element: one is Juan Belmonte, and the other Armillita.

This afternoon it is simmering hot between red-hot earth and steel-hot sky. The seats in the sun are too hot to sit upon without cushions; newcomers provide diversions for their experienced neighbours with little yelps and bounds into the air. Every girl in the town who owns a mantilla wears it in honour of Belmonte; the shawls flame around the boxes; the *sombra* is like a bed of flowers.

All the preliminary ritual is performed with great splendour, great solemnity: a solemnity that reaches its height in the shortest, physically the least significant of the four brilliant figures that walk abreast in the *paseo*. And at last the ring is empty, and we are waiting for the bull . . .

The bulls, on this day at Antequera, are not very good; they are sluggish, and there is one—the second—which is shifty. This, in itself, would excuse the matador, to himself, and to some extent to his public, for a mediocre performance. But it is getting near the end of the season, and all the *aficionados* are agog for a memory to carry them through the dreary days ahead, and for something that will top their reminiscences of the past season.

Whatever the latter-day art of Belmonte may lack of its former glory—and it is because there are many lapses, as well as from a desire not to bore the reader, that I refrain from a rule of thumb commentary on this *corrida*—there is no diminishment of spiritual authority. When the small and lonely figure walks out on the sand, you could hear a pin drop. The long 'jaw of a wolf', as the Spanish call it, is part of a mask, in which the only openings are the dark and empty eye-sockets. Death at his elbow, his shadow by his side: thus it is three people who go out, Death, and Belmonte, and his dark, familiar shadow.

A ghostly troupe of butterflies draws away to the *barrera*, along which each leaning figure can feel the slow beat of his neighbour's heart. And it is like a somnambulist that Belmonte spreads out his cape for the first time and gathers the bull into it, with tenderness—oh, with an infinite tenderness!—and draws the bull and the cape round his body as though both were one.

A sigh breaks from the audience, and shapes itself into an 'Olé!' that sounds like an Amen. Each time he does this, it is like the celebration of a religious rite, and the response of the audience is graver, more fervent, more exalted with each one.

This may be the place to say that among one's most poignant memories of the bullring is the sound of the shouts which, from time to time, proclaim the watchers' interest and their approval or disapproval of the performers. The triple *Olé* which greets three *veronicas* perfectly performed, and are themselves so perfectly timed that they might be conducted by the leader of an orchestra, is unforgettable: as is the quality of the sound itself—deep, primitive, dragged up from the bowels of a race. That triple *Olé* has its inception is the darkness of centuries, and those who give it forth are obeying an instinct implanted in them by their fore-fathers. I have seen a stranger so deeply affected by it that he was obliged to leave his seat, and fainted on the steps that lead to the upper galleries.

One of the *cuadrilla* now takes the bull and turns it back towards the matador, and again the *pas de quatre* is enacted—between Belmonte and his shadow and Death and the bull; and as the *suerte* develops—without brilliance, for the bull does not lend itself to a show of brilliance—the personal tension between the man and the animal increases; and it is this personal and occult struggle, rather than the one that our eyes register, that makes up the greatness of the *corrida*.

He plants no darts; his physical shortcomings have long obliged him to give up handling the banderillas. Armillita goes in, in all his sinister, Aztec beauty, and plants an impeccable pair. It is his best *suerte*. While the *cuadrilla* sees to the others, Belmonte, his eyes on the ring, is taking, still with his sleepwalker's movement, the sword from his assistant, and, after the trumpet has sounded, once more makes his strange, threefold entrance upon the scene.

The bull is very heavy, stubborn, and will not put his feet together; but among the graceless whistles and yells that come from the tiers, Belmonte remains cold, unmoved, and evidently beyond external disturbance. You can hear him speaking quietly, tranquilly to the bull, while the *muleta* describes its slow, crimson arc from left to right; then he goes in, *volapie*, following his sword.

But the sword grinds on bone, is jerked from his hand and flies in a parabola across the sand. Happily, it does not cross the *barrera*, as it did, once[1] . . . Calmly he holds out his hand for another.

When the time comes he does what has to be done with dispatch, without a flicker of haste or doubt, and, above all, without that note of disgusting triumph over a fallen enemy with which I have seen some of the best matadores spoil their conclusions. After four failures, the bull goes quietly on its knees and rolls over in the sand, and

---

[1] At Corunna, 5th August 1934, when a spectator was killed.

Belmonte's smile, as he turns to salute the President's box, is as gentle as though he had just put a child to sleep.

I have seen many performances more brilliant than the one I saw on that sultry Antequera afternoon, but never one so pure, or that preserved so immaculately the integrity of man and beast. That, to me, is the 'great' quality in Belmonte's fighting: that, just as he never lowers himself, he never lowers the animal with whom he fights. I have never seen him employ an unworthy *adorno*, or do anything to disturb the ritual conception of the fight. He is the supreme exponent of the tragic cycle which has passed from generation to generation into the blood-stream of the nation: whose appreciation is bound up in that thing called *pundonor*, for which the English translation, personal honour, is so much less than the equivalent.

We who have watched the spectacle are left drained of energy, as though we had taken physical part in it, and sleep the profound sleep of emotional exhaustion all the way back from Antequera to Granada.

(IV)

NOVILLADA

If one has not yet got one's bullfighting in perspective: to put it plainly, if the *suerte* of the horse still destroys all one's pleasure in it as a spectacle and all one's desire to learn about it as an art—one will get much more enjoyment out of the *novilladas* than out of a *corrida*. That is, if one does not think about them too deeply. It might perhaps enlighten some of the foreign public who cheerfully buy seats for the *novilladas*, while nothing in the world would induce them to see a *corrida*, to know that some of the most experienced bullfighters will pay to enter their sons in the *cuadrilla* of an established matador, rather than to allow them to go through the ruinous and often disastrous experience of fighting the novillada bulls. I have even heard it stated that So-and-so has bought his son the *alternativa*—that is to say, has paid for his launching as a full-fledged matador, to save his spirit being broken and his career ended before it has begun in the *novillada* ring.

I have seen some interesting *novilleros*, but I must admit on the whole not to gaining much pleasure from this spectacle of watching sweating and terrified youths harried round the ring by full-sized bulls, not quite up to *corrida* standard, but, for that very reason, often more tricky and vicious than the bulls the matadores are called upon to handle: bulls which have not been reduced by the *banderilleros'* pikes but which reach the final *suerte* almost as vigorous, and ten times more savage, then when they were let into the ring. I confess to sickening in that moment when the *novillero* takes his sometimes not very first-class sword from the sword-handler, and goes out like David against Goliath on the suddenly lonely patch of sand. After all, David had seven chances . . .

Let me say at once that my views put me in the minority. The crowd—both native and foreign—loves courage; and one may, if one is lucky, see more raw courage in a single *novillada* than in a whole season of *corridas*, for the men and youths fighting in them have their reputations to establish, and, out of sheer desperation, take risks which a matador, without prejudicing his prestige (or disdainful of a prestige he believes to be secure) knows how to avoid.

The most exciting *novilladas* I have seen were in Sevilla, during the month of May: when the fighters were elected by ballot to represent the various *barrios* of the town, and there was naturally a lot of high feeling, one *barrio* barracking the representative of another, hand-to-hand fighting breaking out along the tiers of the *sol*, yells of protest from one gang or another at practically every decision of the President and a veritable storm of cushions, water-bottles, and other missiles descending upon the ring during practically every *suerte*; but the entire audience joining with the most good-hearted unanimity in roars of laughter each time some unlucky youth was scooped up and bumped from vertebra to vertebra down the bull's back, to slump ignominiously off its tail. There was one bull, I remember, a red one, which specialized in this circus trick; with its rather short, curved horns it just hooked the man over its head and bucked him down its spine. It did this three, or perhaps four times, each time to the accompaniment of rapturous yells from the audience. My companion was almost unconscious: he sat, rolling from side to side, mopping the water out of his eyes, while I tried to guess at the injuries of the boy who was being carried out of the ring by two of his companions.

I suppose the *novilladas* compare with the *corrida* something as village cricket compares with the game at Lord's; they are certainly brighter, on the whole, and an English friend whom, having been disgusted with the *corrida*, I persuaded to see a *novillada*, enjoyed the experience immensely. It happened to be a good *novillada*, with two very interesting little boys, grandsons of the keeper of the Malaga ring. The contrast between the two brothers, neither of whom was more than fifteen, was most amusing to watch; one, the smaller and sallower of the two, was, to begin with, sick with fear—no matter of shame, for I have seen matadores who, apparently, regard this as part of the ritual of entering the ring; while the other, radiant, volatile, teeth glittering in an enchanting grin, pranced in immediately to engage the bull in a series of by no means contemptible *adornos*. It was interesting, however, as the fight went on, to see how this grin faded, the cheerful face lost its colour and began to turn dusty grey, the movements of the cape became more snatched and desperate—when the other brother, who, up to then, had hardly left the *barera*, on which he hung almost like one prepared to abandon consciousness, slowly straightened himself, walked out stiff-kneed, and opened out his cape with a solemnity recalling the Master himself. From that moment the fight belonged to this boy, although the other, reassured by his brother's presence, made quick recovery; but his part, from now on, was that of the acolyte, waiting upon the high priest.

I fear the civil war cut short the careers of this promising couple, of whom I have heard nothing since I left Spain just before the outbreak.

The attraction of the *novilladas* is, of course, for the *aficion*, the chance of spotting or of following some future star of the ring; they are very important, for there the bull-fighter earns, in the most desperate and dangerous fashion, his right to wear the long cape of the matador. Many *novilleros* never reach that altitude; many are condemned, year after year, for a pittance that is barely sufficient to pay their expenses, to face the ordeal of a recurring death-in-life: with the knowledge that, at the end of it, if death does not intervene, their almost inevitable lot is maiming and poverty. Why do they do it? God knows.

I have heard it said that the bullring gets hold of a man as the theatre gets hold of him; he may loathe it, but he cannot tear himself away from it. I doubt it, having known a good number of bullfighters. I am sure that if one were to offer any bullfighter I have met (not excluding *all* of the stars) an income for life, he would turn his back with thankfulness on the ring, and never revisit it, except, perhaps, to bask in the envy of his less fortunate colleagues, on the other side of the *barrera*.

Vanity has something—a good deal—to do with it, and the hope that is said to spring eternal in the human breast—that one day he will strike lucky: that one glorious afternoon will see him receiving the sword from the hands of Marcial in the ring at Madrid: that from thenceforward his life will be that triumphal procession of Rolls Royces, women's favours, extravagance and luxury which is the life of the successful matador. Without this hope in his breast, it is my perhaps mistaken belief that the average *novillero* would commit suicide—which reminds me that I have never heard of a bullfighter committing suicide, excepting accidentally, by some folly in the ring. Another reason for his not quitting is probably that inadaptability, common to artists of all kinds, to the common issues of earning a living.

Successful bullfighters retire, and turn, very often, into excellent business men; but the *novillero* has no capital with which to set up a business. The colourless drudgery of working for other people does not appeal to him. But he has to live, so he continues to sell his brains, his nerves and his physique for the little they are worth until these fail him.

Perhaps this explains a little while I, personally, find the *novilladas* gloomy, unless there is some particularly hopeful beginner on whom to fix my attention. And, even then, I cannot help wondering how much chance he has: whether he has any rich backer to help him to exploit his talents . . . This is, of course, quite the wrong way to look at *novilladas*, so perhaps this section of the chapter had better not have been written.

CHAPTER XIII

FLAMENCO

No monument left by the Moorish race testifies to the inextinguishable quality of the Moorish *ethos* to the same extent as the flamenco, that wild and occult echo of strains that rang from the ramparts of the Alhambra ten centuries ago; and—this is significant—although every Andalusían child almost before it can talk, produces as unconsciously as a bird some phrase that derives from the Moorish pattern, I have never met any foreigner, even among those domiciled in Spain, who could even begin to sing flamenco. They are too elusive, too alien to our northern ear—those sliding semitones, those seemingly endless cadenzas that break off exactly where one has begun to anticipate the next phrase, that have no recognizable time-unit and nothing, apparently, but the singer's want of breath to prevent their continuing to eternity.

The beautiful word flamenco, as frequently misused as it is misunderstood by the foreigner, who, for the most part, assumes (incorrectly) that it stands for gitano, owes its inclusion in the Spanish language to the Flemish settlers in the northern provinces, whose language and customs, so different from those of the natives, became synonymous with all that was odd, bizarre or exotic in the whole of Spain. Thus the word flamenco, coined for the strangers, came to mean foreign, or fantastic, and was applied equally to all in conduct, speech or art that did not conform to the accepted norm. It is common in Andalucía to hear someone whose behaviour is eccentric or amusing described as '*muy flamenco*'—a description which implies flattery, rather than adverse criticism, for, to be 'flamenco', one must display spirit, independence and, above all, that 'saltiness' that the Andalucían adores.

If the gipsies are 'flamenco', it is not because they are gipsies, but because their style of dressing, their dance and their affranchised behaviour single them out as a highly individualized race.

With the passage of time, however, the word has been associated more and more exclusively with a certain type of singing, and with the closely related arts of music and the dance: so that it is now taken for granted, unless the context forbids, that, in speaking of flamenco, one refers to one or other of these arts, which reach their fullest and richest expression in Andalucía.

I first encountered flamenco on a moonlight night in Granada, when, with an American companion, I had just come out of the only cabaret Granada boasted. Let it be said, once and for all, that Spanish cabarets are very bad. I was in a mood of disgust and disgruntlement, and reproached my companion with the waste of one of the few nights left to me in Granada. And, suddenly, there was the sound of a guitar.

Briefly, we were invited by a party of gentlemen who had engaged the *patio* of a neighbouring tavern for a night of flamenco to join their company, and thus I heard my first flamenco singing, and first met Francisco Gálvez Gómez.

Here indeed was the pattern of the great amateur of flamenco and of the Andalucían gentleman: a creature of the sun, inevitably attracting all that is gay, honest, generous and wholesome to his vicinity. Short, broad, fair rather than dark, with the grey Granadino eye alert with humour, Frasquito, as he was generally known, was a popular hero, and knew it; not in the unpleasant sense of personal vanity, but of looking upon it as rather a serious responsibility.

The next morning, my American acquaintance left, but I was determined, even if it meant sacrificing my reservations, to hear more flamenco before returning to England. Elementary as was my Spanish, I had managed to convey this determination of mine to Frasquito, and it was he who arranged that I should hear it, the next time, under the most perfect conditions that could be found for the enhancement of the experience.

Again the moon was staring white. Frasquito and I sat, necessarily mute, in opposite corners of the big car, with Enrique the guide to act, when needed, as interpreter, and a gipsy guitarrista mounted beside the chauffeur; and, as we shot down beneath the elms, across the blazing Plaza Nueva and into the narrow causeway that follows the bed of the Darro, instinct told me that I was to have one of the strangest, perhaps the most poignant experiences of my life.

Soon we were mounting, by cobbled ways, between high white façades that seemed to rock towards us with each lurch of the car, to emerge on a rough track that ran like a gallery round the steep sides of what I was later to know as the Sacromonte. Frasquito said something, and the guide translated: 'Señor Gálvez tells you not yet to look out to your right.'

Obediently I fixed my eyes on the dark hillside, where flashed now and then a white building, a gleam of orange light from a window; a sensation of curious remoteness, of total separation from everything familiar was enhanced by the dark faces which, now and again, as we mounted slowly, pressed themselves close to the windows of the car. Presently we drew up before a little blind white house, closely shuttered, upon whose warped olivewood door the chauffeur knocked in a fashion that was evidently a signal. After a long while, there was the noise of bolts being drawn, a key turned, and from the black cavern of the open door a troglodyte stepped into the moonlight, a dwarfish figure with its head bandaged with a black scarf, who made mute signs to us to enter.

Someone—Frasquito or the guide—struck a match, and there was a flight of broken stairs. For a second—let's admit it—I hesitated; then the firm clasp of Frasquito's hand resolved my hesitation. The match burned out: we mounted silently, in the darkness.

Never, until they put the pennies on my eyes, shall I forget the scene that lay before me when we stepped out on the broad terrace. I knew at once why Frasquito had bidden me not to look to the right. There was the great white moon, the blazing stars in a cloudless sky, and opposite, across the black ravine in whose depths meanders the uncertain streak of the Darro, the Alhambra itself, its massive towers all silvered, all transformed in a splendour of moonlight. The silence was so complete that we could hear the nightingales across the valley, and the faint chuckle of the Darro over its stony bed.

The guide and the gipsy were dismissed to some little artificial arbour fashioned out of pots of bamboo. All was foreseen, all arranged, from the perfect setting to the waiter who came out presently with the wine in its tubs of ice, with cigarettes, with olives, with the trays of *turron*—most delectable of sweetmeats. Easy chairs, cushions, a shawl and a fan—nothing was forgotten; never was anything so thoughtfully planned, so carefully executed.

We had no use for the interpreter that night. In some curious fashion, I found I could understand my host, and he me; we talked in our own languages, without pause, without embarrassment—without, I believe, ever remembering that the shape and sounds of our words were not the same, or even realizing that the dawn would transport us each back to our own mute prisons.

When Frasquito sang, the hillsides held their breath, the stars ceased twinkling and burned with a calm, low light; looking over the parapet, I saw, gathered under our walls, a soft, dark multitude of gipsies stolen from their caves, of Albaicin dwellers drawn from their sleep—drawn by a voice like a golden trumpet, whose echoes blended with their hushed '*Oles*'.

I was to hear that voice many times, over a period of four years; and always it was to give me an indescribable sense of all that was strange, beautiful and inapprehensible to human knowledge, to stir me with its intimations of the past and forgotten, its imperious yet nameless summons . . . But to this day I do not know which was the little house to which I was taken that night, to receive my initiation into the mysteries of flamenco. In all our many excursions, we never went there again; and this I felt was as it should be, for there could be no recapturing of so emotional an experience.

What, it may be asked, are the qualities that make a flamenco singer?

It is not a matter of voice, for at a *concurso de flamenco* that I attended, when Frasquito was a judge, the first place was awarded to a woman whose thin thread of vocal sound was hardly audible beyond the judges' platform, and must have been wholly inaudible from the farther galleries. Like all flamenco singers, she sat to sing; she leaned her forehead on her hand, as though she were weeping.

The necessary technical equipment consists, apparently, in excessive flexibility of the vocal cords, and an almost superhuman control of the diaphragm muscle, so that the breath remains boxed in the thoracic cavity as long as it pleases the singer to continue his cadenza—which is a matter dependent entirely on his inspiration and his skill.

But the true art of the flamenco rests in the inspiration itself: in the richness and variety of the improvisation and in its emotional content. There is also the curious, occult liaison which establishes itself between the singer and the past, the singer and his accompanist. To make sure of this liaison, it is common for the singer to rest his hand on the accompanist's knee or shoulder, to lean towards him, or to press his foot against the other's. No signs are exchanged; it is purely a matter of contact, of making a channel for the communication of the singer's intention to the player's mind. Sometimes the channel is unnecessary; the two sit apart, even turned from each other, and some of the singer's postures and movements are curious in the extreme.

It can hardly be sufficiently emphasized that in true flamenco singing there is no element whatever of the theatrical; that therefore all flamenco performances that take place in the theatre lose quality, are falsified and altogether inferior to what one may hear in the *patio*, in the tavern, in the garden or the cave.

The state of flamenco singing is a state of trance; a state of spiritual withdrawal, in which the singer sinks deep within himself, and becomes less and less conscious of his audience. The effect, at the height of the performance, might almost be described as mediumistic: the eyes close, or become set and vacant, an expression of torment distorts the features, which drain themselves of colour, even to the lips. The singer bends, writhes, doubles his body as though suffering an excruciating torture; the sweat glistens on his brow, an arm curves itself strangely, the fingers crisped, as though in the act of tearing something out of the singer's soul.

The gipsies are exceptions to this almost general rule; a gipsy sits upright, well forward on the chair, knees wide apart, chest lifted, head thrown back and arms akimbo, with hands planted on the upper thigh. It is a splendid attitude, proud, free, impressive—and theatrical; and although I have heard many gipsy voices (especially among the women) of a magnificent brazen sonority, it is the theatrical element, characteristic of the race, which explains—to me—why I have never heard a first class gipsy flamenco singer.

Almost without exception, any amateur is better than any professional of the flamenco. The highly paid professionals, such as Niño de Marchena, or Niña de las Peinas, have long since sacrificed their artistic integrity to the demands of their public. Performing three or four times a week in the theatres, their art has become mechanical, and it is very rarely that one hears from them anything that can compare with the singing that takes place in private, among a band of friends. From the very nature of the performance, it is bound to be so.

All flamenco singing is an improvisation; therefore you never hear the same song sung twice in exactly the same way. The words, which are sometimes traditional, more often modern, are composed by local poets and often sold in the streets, on thin pink or green sheets, for a few centimos. The singers buy, memorize them and use them as a basis for their improvisations. In a Granada tavern I met a priest who composed and wrote out for me, there and then, the beautiful little *solea* in the Andaluz dialect which Francisco Gálvez Gómez sang for me the same night in Luisa's *patio*:

'Anda ve y dile a tu mare
Que to tuvo en mis brazos
Parte de una madruga.'

('Go tell thy mother that I held thee in my arms until the coming of the dawn.')

The words of the flamenco express, in the minimum of lines, usually some sentiment simple to the point of näiveté: regret for a lost mistress, a dead mother; a girl watering the pot plants on her balcony; a caged bird; the beauty of the town or countryside; religious devotion. The songs themselves fall into classes, of which, from the foreigner's point of view, the fandangos and fandangillos are probably the most diverting, with their rough *brio*, to which contributes, not only the guitar but the much louder, more startling bandurría. These songs are very noisy, very gay, and usually serve to 'warm up' the atmosphere and to establish the current of good fellowship upon which the success of the evening depends. In particular, they lend themselves to dancing, and, if there is a gipsy present, it is during the fandangillo that she will stride forward, to take up her insolent posture, to loud cries of '*Olé, la gitana!*'—'*Anda!*'—'*Guapísima!*'

The jerk of the head, the shaking of shoulders and breasts, the frenzied roll of the hips, snapping of the fingers, rattling of high heels and serpent-like bending of the body are followed with growing excitement by the audience, which contributes to and emphasizes the rhythm with hand clapping. One thing is certain—that however discreetly the dancing may begin, it will by the end of the evening have reached a pitch of lively obscenity, gestures losing their classic formality and becoming more and more broadly specific, and the phallic significance of the dance emerging with the gradual absorption of the spectators into the spirit of the performance.

The fandangillos, together with the regional forms, such as the granadinas and malagueñas, are part of the repertory of every flamenco singer. My dear friend, blind Manuel of the Albaicín, sings granadinas more exquisitely than anyone I have ever heard: in a thin voice of celestial purity which passes every now and then into silence as his breath fails him, but holds a quality of ecstasy which puts it quite outside the limits of technical criticism. Another excellent singer of the *granadina* is a young ex-bullfighter, who, having taken the *cornada* early in his career, seems to pour all the sadness and frustration of his soul into his song. But whereas his is a tortured and agonized rendering, Manuel lifts up his fine head and his sweet blind eyes, and makes of his singing an act of praise and beatitude, of belief in and devotion to the Virgin of the Angustias whose miraculous image he has never seen.

The test of the flamenco singer comes with the *solea*, whose grave and classic character demands altogether another calibre of interpretation. *Soleas* are not given, except by request, to foreign audiences, which, it is taken for granted, neither appreciate nor respect their recondite qualities. This was amusingly demonstrated to me when, having arranged for a flamenco evening at a certain price, my host was asked for a hundred pesetas more than the agreed fee. When, naturally, he protested, the naïve explanation was forthcoming, that the singers had only expected to give the usual range of subjects which had proved acceptable to foreigners, but that the señora had asked for soleas and martinetes!

I was obliged to assure my (English) host that this was reasonable: that for an evening of regional songs and jotas, we would probably have done just as well by calling in the garden boy, and the men who drove up the asses with the water and bread, but that it takes a true artist to perform the solea, and that my request for soleas rose partly out of my curiosity about the artistic equipment of our performers. Which explanation, I may add, was accepted with excellent grace; they got their extra pesetas, and more bottles of wine were opened, to the glory and honour of flamenco. (I *did* prevent my host's being victimized to the extent of another fifty pesetas for a supposedly torn dress, which is a common gipsy trick, played with more or less success when gipsies are engaged to perform in private houses.)

The *martinete* is my favourite flamenco form, but I have only once heard it sung well, and it was on this particular evening. This song of the chain-gang prisoners, unlike most of the song-forms, has many verses; it is almost alarming, as the song progresses, to watch its effect on the singer. His eyes sink back in his head, the skin tightens on his face, becomes livid; gradually he slips sidelong in his chair, his hands fall lifeless, the knuckles trailing on the ground; his voice fades . . . a singular instance of the projection of the singer's personality into the character his song embodies.

A word must be said on the accompanist. The guitar, it must be known, is the study of a life-time, and there are very few good accompanists of flamenco. The gipsies, who are brilliant but abominably careless executants, and who often own indifferent instruments, are too insolent, too anxious to exploit their own personalities, to demonstrate their own accomplishments, to make good accompanists. They will, without conscience, sacrifice the singer to their own performances; their technique is rough, without subtlety, and, if reprimanded or criticized, they turn sullen. They are most successful as soloists, or in playing for dancing.

Whatever are the ordinary qualities of a good 'straight' accompanist, the accompanist of flamenco must possess *in excelsis*. Apart from command of his instrument, and an endless gift for improvisation, he must have the personal qualities of intuition, of initiative and of diffidence which must never degenerate into uncertainty. He must be prepared in every instance to subordinate his own creative genius to the requirements of the singer, and his mind must be sensitive enough always to anticipate a change of key, of tempo or of mood.

It was the possession of all these qualities that made 'Miguel el Santo' almost an ideal accompanist: I say 'almost', because his very delicacy defeated him in the rougher, wilder music. When I first knew Francisco Gálvez Gómez, he employed a gipsy, whose power and fantasy in the fandangillos I have never heard equalled, let alone surpassed; but in accompanying the *soleas*, and even in some of the regional music, he displayed a coarseness and vulgarity not to be endured. He proved, as time went on, so impossible a person, so over-persuaded of his own importance, that Frasquito got rid of him, and took instead the gentle, humble Miguel, who had been a pupil of Segovia, and whose nickname, 'El Santo', expressed, not only his religious devotion to his music, but the purity and austerity of character for which all who knew loved and respected him.

The dramatic and spectacular quality of flamenco dancing lend it a universal appeal, made up partly of the movements themselves, partly of the gowns, the magentas, scarlets and chrome yellows, in which the dancers deck themselves, and partly of the sparkling vigour of the gipsies who are its chief exponents.

Again, one rarely sees the pure art of flamenco dancing on the stage, where modifications and sophistications creep in; where the dancers lose their primitive honesty and are affected by an audience and surroundings so different from those to which they are accustomed; yet what survives in the theatre bears its transplantation well, on the whole, being evidently a hardier growth than the song and the instrumental music.

Almost all the young gipsy girls dance as they breathe—with a grace and subtlety quite entrancing: every movement natural as the opening of a flower, the Oriental flexibility of wrists and insteps lending a fluidity, as of running water, to all their attitudes. From point of view of technical accomplishment, the men are probably the best dancers: it is they who provide the spectators with the most authentic and straightforward sensation, with their leaps, their drumming heels, their tremendous attack and the resilience which comes from thighs of steel.

But to get the full flavour of the dance, there is nothing to equal the middle-aged women. From those heavy-seeming bosoms and haunches, that yet are soft and lithe as serpents, is distilled such a wealth of artifice, of experience and suggestion, that the performances of the girls seem frail in comparison; those beautiful, hard, ravaged faces lend themselves to emotions that are not within the range of youth.

Perhaps it is the mere fact of knowing that their hours as dancers are numbered that brings the note of fever, of morbidity, of decadence into their dancing, which heightens its emotional effect.

We have spoken briefly of the guitar—'the soul of Andalucía'—and of the bandurría; the third instrument of the flamenco orchestra is not to be ignored—the castañettas which flutter between the dancers' fingers, or are rattled by the onlookers at a flamenco gathering.

These small, shallow cups of polished wood, that are looped by their silken cords to the players' fingers, vary in size and quality of tone—the latter according to the wood of which they are made. The ones sold to tourists, and made often of real or imitation ebony, are usually badly balanced and of inferior quality; above all, they are new, which means they can never produce the delicate variations of tone that come from those which have, perhaps, been handed down through five or six generations. I have handled a little pair of olivewood castañettas, more than a hundred years old, whose surface was worn to satin, and whose twin cups, hardly thicker than shells, chuckled as softly as a nestful of sparrows. Such fragile instruments do not find favour with the gipsies, who choose in preference the larger, louder, harsher varieties that contribute the maximum of noise—and therefore, to their way of thinking, of excitement—to the performance.

There is no limit to the variety of sound and of meaning that a skilled performer—of whom, without doubt, the greatest was La Argentina—can extract from the castañettas; the majority use them merely as a means of emphasizing the rhythm. Actually, they are as much of a life study as the guitar, and, in a hundred performances, you are lucky if you come across a good one.

A young rival to La Argentina, calling herself Argentinita, had made her appearance about the time of my first visit to Spain. After hearing her, I had the curiosity to buy two records of the same piece of music, the popular *Danza*, by Granados, of which the castañetta solo was played, in the one case by La Argentina, in the other by

Argentinita. These two records admirably exemplify the distinction between the performance of genius and another who relies for her reputation on youthful bravura and vitality. The crudely brilliant performance of Argentinita does not bear a moment's comparison with the suave, thoughtful and infinitely varied rendering of her great rival.

CHAPTER XIV

'GITANA'

ALL up and down the Generalife hill, outside 'El Waashinton' and along the campo de los Martires, swoops a flight of butterflies. Without them, the Granada scene is incomplete. Entrancing to the eye, soft-voiced, cajoling, importunate and wholly exasperating—they haunt the Alhambra precincts. Over their sleek heads, their lovely olive brows on which are plastered ringlets that look as though they had been painted on with a fine brush, nod the carnations; their flounces of magenta and orange, crimson, vermilion and purple, make eddies in the dust. They will offer you a fan, a pair of clumsy castañettas (the best are not to be bought); they will press a carnation into your hand with a murmured *'Guapa!'*, and shadow you softly until they have extracted payment for the unsolicited compliment. They will—it goes without saying—offer to tell your fortune . . .

To the life of Granada the gipsies are what the plumbago and the morning glory and the tiny yellow roses they call *'petimini'* are to its rust-coloured stones; they are the grace-notes on its sombre motif. And so long as one is content to leave them as such, they are harmless.

> 'My mother said that I never should
> Play with the gipsies in the wood'—

a sound axiom for the average gringo. I have never met, or heard of, any countryman (or countrywoman) of my own, with the single exception of Augustus John, whose claim to 'knowing' the Spanish gipsies bears even a casual investigation. The gipsies themselves are really hilariously funny about it. Although few can read, none speak our language, and all are dependent for their foreign news upon the mysterious grapevine that links tribe to tribe over the length and breadth of our continent—they are sufficiently informed to laugh to the echoes the pretensions of any gringo rash enough to attempt to reduce them to a literary formula.

Which is not to say I have never 'known' gipsies: spent delightful evenings in their company, enjoyed the expensive honour of sponsoring their babies and danced at their weddings. And at the end of all the *burlería* I have just enough sense left to realize that none of these experiences entitles me to take the verb To Know out of inverted commas, or to profess familiarity with a society of which I have touched no more than the fringe.

Taking it by and large, I would say that associations between gipsy and non-gipsy people—when they depart from the well-defined pattern laid down by guides and tourists since the inception of *turismo*—are seldom productive of anything but misunderstandings, and of a sourness that rankles on both sides; for the very simple reason that, sooner or later, the gringo is bound to expect of the gipsy principles which do not come within the scope of gipsy mentality, while the gipsy feels himself betrayed when the hitherto sympathetic gringo digs his heels in over some trifle which—until it was pointed out to him—no right-minded gipsy has ever regarded as having any importance whatever in the social scheme. *En somme:* our contempt for gipsy morality is no less deep than his contempt for ours; and, unless we accept that premise, it is pure folly to overstep the conventional limits of inter-racial amenities.

Nor is it anything but affectation for the gringo who has not, as a preliminary, mastered the Calo language, to pretend that he (or she) knows anything at all about the Spanish gipsies; sympathy (which, boiled down, is little more than sentiment) is, most emphatically, not enough.

Heaven forbid, therefore, that I should write about gipsies in anything but a strictly objective spirit. My friend (dare I, for once, omit the inverted commas?), Paca, approves of this attitude: as she approves of my wholly noncommittal attitude to her people—Paca, who dances the summer nights out and starves through the winter to keep her two children in boarding school in Malaga: who even accepts that final degradation of the true gipsy, cabaret work, in order that her little Carmencita and Manuela should learn what Paca herself has never learned—to read the printed word.

Paca, who is fat, may be thirty years of age and looks fifty, is remarkably ugly, and is the best dancer on the Sacromonte, agrees with me that the gap between gringo and gipsy is no less wide and deep than that between the white and the coloured races: deeper, in some respects, for it is easier for an African Negro, for example, in continuous touch with white civilization, to assimilate the standards, both moral and material, of that civilization, than it is for a gipsy to dispose of the centuries of tradition which have given the race its present form: which has maintained its purity through the force of the inter-tribal taboo against marriage away from the gipsy stock.

Typical of the mental confusion in gringo-gipsy relationships is a saying that seems to have passed into local currency: 'The gipsies are the romance of Granada.' If so, it is romance on a tuppence-coloured pattern.

The Granadino gipsies, in their electrically lit caves on the Sacromonte, are the aristocracy of the Spanish tribes. Totally currupted by the tourist population, in them all the charm, the venality and the viciousness of the gipsy reaches its apotheosis; they are even more sophisticated than their relatives in Sevilla, the inhabitants of the suburb of Triana, who contribute to the programmes at the Kursaal, and entertain gay parties to music and pink champagne in the little private rooms behind the proscenium arch. In Granada you will not be offered pink champagne, because it is not '*tipico*', and Granada is fully alive to the fact that to be '*tipico*' is good business: such good business that La Riva, which you may buy for fourteen pesetas, within a few yards, in the Albaicin, can fetch as much as thirty-five pesetas a bottle on the Sacromonte.

These Granadino gipsies, *de luxe* edition of a race that flourishes throughout the length and breadth of Spain—

well, perhaps the word 'flourishes' is an exaggeration: there is little 'flourishing' about those miserables one meets on the long roads of the north, forbidden entry to certain towns, sending their naked offspring to beg by the waysides: the problem of whose existence is insoluble by anyone who gives it a thought—these Granadino gipsies know all about Hollywood; know the vast sums that foreign impresarios have been known to pay a flamenco dancer; know the exact value of their posturings to the artists who frequently engage them to sit; know their importance in the economics of a town that depends for an appreciable portion of its revenue on tourists.

And the curious effect of this knowledge is to make them not less, but more, 'bonafidely' gipsy: to accentuate those characteristics which are most truly of their kind—pulchritude, grace, cunning, occultism, for which their reputation is world-wide. Whatever makes a gipsy, these have, *in excelsis:* and it is a pity for those, who, beguiled by their glittering charm, forget what underlies it. As a tourist, one can afford to disregard this *fond*, and to make the most of the sparkle they bring into a morbid and even enervating air; but the position of the inhabitant is different.

It would disconcert some of the villa dwellers to know how much of their private lives is an open book to the Sacromente. How this comes about it would be difficult to say; it is positive, however, that the gipsy who turns up at your *cancela* with the usual bright-eyed whine for alms will depart with more than the few *gordas* you contribute for the sake of the small, human monkey wrapped in her shawl. Your *rejas* may be proof against a gipsy's fingers; nothing is proof against her predatory eyes, and a little of your private life will depart with her down the dusty pathway. Your servants—who, as a rule, detest her—may refuse her access to your premises, even, on the sly, set the dogs on her: those eyes will possess themselves of some shreds of your secrecy, even in the instant of flight.

In short—you may hate the gipsies, lose your temper with them, execrate them and repel their advances—the one thing you cannot, if you are a Granadino, is ignore them. They know everything, and their discretion is to be bought

—at a price. In very rare instances it may be exercised on behalf of someone who has gained (sometimes in some completely unconscious way) their goodwill. And it is policy to pay, without complaint, that tiny monthly blackmail that purchases immunity from the tedious highwaymanry of the hill. They keep to their bargain scrupulously; no one who gives that handful of monthly coppers is ever pestered, and heedless little boys and girls are sharply called off, if they infringe the privilege created by their elders. No one murmurs '*Guapa!*' or presses a flower in your hand . . . and there is, oddly enough, something a little depressing in such immunity.

'Put away your handbag; these people are not to be trusted.' 'Do not smile so much at that woman; she will take advantage of you.' Such exhortations might be prompted by self-interest, if Paca had ever made a *perra chica* out of them. But, for her own inscrutable reasons, she has taken me under her wing, and I find it politic to let anything I hear or see of gipsy behaviour filter through Paca's intelligence before drawing conclusions.

She is the only gipsy I have known to refuse money and *to mean it*. The rule is, to refuse it when offered, and wait the opportunity to steal it; so long as one knows the rule, no harm is done on either side. Once, knowing Paca had had a bad week, and had been treated meanly by the tourists, I told Luisa to give her a few duros. The following week, when she happened to do well, Paca paid me back. Not in cash, but in kind: two fowls for the pot. Stolen? One is not so indelicate as to probe such matters.

Paca and I sit on the steps, while she mends one of those innumerable petticoats of broderie anglaise that puff out the flounces of the dancing frocks. On a spring morning, the earth all round and about the caves is snowy with body-linen, bleaching in the sun: for there is no one more immaculate in her person that a Granada gipsy. I have seen chests of linen fine enough for a bride's trousseau, worn habitually by these dwellers on the hill.

We sit in the sun, exchanging—not without difficulty— bits of gossip; Paca knows more Calo than Andaluz, my

Andaluzis halting, and, despite Paca's best efforts and her ceaseless mockery, I have learned but a few words of Calo. But scraps of information seep through, and I get strange flashes of enlightenment on my Alhambra neighbours and my compatriots that give me, at times, the guilty thrill of peeping through a keyhole. Of married couples, Paca knows all about which is unfaithful, and with whom; she knows the politics of each kitchen; she knows the squalor underlying an outward pomp, and the jealously guarded secrets of Doña Cataluña's false toupee and the sensational thrust of the young Señora de Tal's bosom. As the sun, and our confidence, warm up, she relates, with gleeful malice, the well-known history of the rich Englishman who fell in love with a gipsy girl: and, regardless of the disrepute into which a gipsy falls among her own people if she marries away from the tribe, induced her to marry him. She describes, in rich detail, the locust descent of the girl's family upon the married couple; the final reduction of the luckless bridegroom to penury and madness and the triumphant return of the girl to her gipsy lover. All this Paca tells with a cheery absence of bias, but keen appreciation of the dramatic values of the narrative. According to her, no gipsy ever loved a gringo save for what she got out of him. There is the story of the young Spaniard who made a gipsy girl his mistress, covered her with jewels—and what happened to him has no fit place in these discreet pages. All these things come out, in the dappled shade of the bougainvillea, threaded with the continual movement of humming-bird moths.

Paca, among her other virtues, has the rare one—among her people—of artistic integrity. Even to the tourists—the nervous, elderly spinsters and naïve provincials who pay fifteen pesetas apiece to see 'some dancing' in the safe surroundings of 'El Waashinton'—I have never seen her give less than her best. All gipsies have an enormous, malicious sense of humour, very subtle and very insolent. A gipsy giving an imitation of a gipsy dance is the quintessence of clowning; the pity is, it is seldom recognized as such! They are perhaps wise, those good little followers of the beaten tracks of *turismo*, to save their pockets at the price of their experience. Gipsy boredom, gipsy humour, gipsy devil, can be very uncomfortable.

'By the way, Paca—thank you for the lovely bunch of *nardo*.'

Paca receives this with a majestic bend of the head; neither of us is ill-bred enough to mention that in the heart of the bouquet, deeply bedded in the perfumed wax of blossoms, was my stolen fan—stolen a week ago on a shopping expedition in the Reyes Católicos. Why should my fan —incidentally, not one of my usual 'shopping' fans, but one of the most treasured specimens of my collection—lost in the strongholds of bourgeois Granada, come back to me via the Sacromonte?—and why should a string of 'culture' pearls, that must have slipped off my neck in one of the taxis, reappear coiled round the foot of my *chato* of manzanilla, in Luisa's tavern? No one was there to claim a reward: only Luisa, sparkling with delight at my surprise.

This is the kind of thing that makes me disclaim any knowledge of the gipsies: that preserves me, at any rate, from generalizations about gipsy morals, which, when one comes to work them out, are completely at the mercy of gipsy whim or gipsy sentiment. And because a gipsy has a kind of guarded liking for you, it by no means follows that she will treat you honestly (according to your gringo pattern): from which, if the liking be mutual, the wholesome lesson may be learned—to take the good and let the rest slide, without fussing. This idea—let's face it—is very difficult of assimilation for the public-schoolminded gringo, and unless one is prepared to swallow it whole, like an oyster, it is better to forget it.

'Did Maruja come to you for the money for the *boda*?'— Tomorrow night there is a wedding party; let no gringo who is invited to a gipsy wedding feel too flattered by the invitation. Its sole reason is to secure the presence of someone who will stand security for the main part of the refreshment. I wink at Paca, who roars with laughter and winks back at me.

'I am arriving at eleven o'clock, in the car of Pepillo, who is Maruja's cousin, and I am bringing the wine; so there is no reason for Maruja to worry, no reason at all,' I assure her. Paca's somewhat thoughtful look betrays her doubt whether I have not profited a little too thoroughly from her teaching; for, of course, the formula is, in this case, to make a present of a hundred, or two hundred, or three hundred—according to one's means and one's generosity—pesetas, 'for the wine'. On the guest's arrival, splendours of floral decoration, clusters of sparkling glass meet the eye; a thimbleful of manzanilla, perhaps, is passed round, in earnest of the feast to come; but the wine——? 'For so many guests we had to buy the wineglasses!' It is difficult—in fact, impossible, to ignore the bright confidence that accepts, as a matter of course, one's readiness to repair the omission. For one person obstinate or boorish enough to stand by his original contribution, a dozen, out of embarrassment or because they are complimented by being invited, fall for the simple jest; more money passes between guests and hosts—and all goes merrily as a marriage bell. No one notices the glasses as they are spirited, a few at a time, back to the neighbouring tavern from which they were borrowed, and, it goes without saying, no one questions the bill—whose total, before the party ends, will certainly have reached a sum that would feast Granada, had all its inhabitants been invited.

This is the kind of thing which, as I have pointed out to Paca, sours our relationships with the gipsies in Granada; and her reply to it, of course, is perfect. 'Why should we put ourselves out to entertain people who are rude to us and call us by bad names unless they pay for it?'

Too often, one fears, the recollection of a matchless spectacle, of a truly exotic experience, is blurred, for the foreigner, by its sordid ending. 'My mother said I never should . . .' And yet——

On the night after I was frightened, in my little carmen, and, I suppose, my servants had sent the tale round, a gipsy boy came, unbidden, to sleep in my porch, within earshot, if wanted, of my call. On the day I had bad news from England, it was a gipsy who brought blind Manuel all the way from the Albaicin, and bade him lift his sweet, unearthly voice in that invocation of the Angustias which is more than any prayer.

Granada is not Granada to me without that dark assembly whose movements are as the trembling of its leaves, its wild and brazen music rival to its nightingales, its intractable gaiety infused with the melancholy of the Moor's last sigh and whose beauty, silver-crowned with sierra snows, is so woven into the beauty of the scene, to which it belongs, as strands of silk in an historic tapestry, that each is inseparable from the other.

Choose as they may to vulgarize themselves for the benefit of the foreigner, the general effect is not a vulgar one: it is only made so by those who, out of ignorance, attempt to invest them with the false romantic. Each of these figures which adorns the highroad, with her flounces and shawl, her combs of jade-green and magenta thrust into the black skein of her hair, has her mean, sly, treacherous male lurking behind her; each wears in her bosom the secret that makes a princess of her—the secret of her immense contempt for the foreigner whose simplicity it is her lifework to exploit.

For her, the clouds and the stars, the falling of a leaf, the breaking of a twig are eloquent. Unable to write, she can, by the disposition of a stone or two, a scrap of tree bark, a crooked flower stalk, leave a message that can be read, not only by the one for whom it was intended, but by any of her race in any part of the globe. She recognizes a message, a warning, or a lover's assignation in a little heap of dust. Beside her immense and savage sophistication, civilization itself seems naïve.

The strong air lifts and scatters them in bright confetti over the dusty earth; they stain the Spring green with the colours of blood, and leave their dark profiles in umber shadow on a rust-red wall. Their green-olive faces, olive-shaped, steal colour from the leaves among which they thrust their flat heads of snakes, with the peacock crests of carnations above their brows: float in the motionless, steel-black water of a tank: peer from the folds of the immense robe of Nuestra Señora de las Angustias. They are not to be known. You can buy everything from a gipsy but knowledge. That they hold in their breasts, and inside their flat snake heads, and in the palms of their small, metallic hands.

    'Oh, city of gipsy folk!
    Who has seen thee and not remembered thee?
    Let them seek thee in my forehead,
    In the playing of moon and sand.'
              (*Garcia Lorca, tr. by W. F. Stirling.*)

CHAPTER XV

THE INNOCENT DEATH

IN MEMORIAM

THERE is shade under a wall, and men rest there, and wonder why the soil is kind to their feet and weariness slips from their limbs like water, and they read love in the faces of their companions, and there is a sweetness of myrrh. For here, in a summer dawn, was spilt the blood of Federico García Lorca, in one of those tulip dawns that are like a cenotaph hung with silk for the triumphant Dead.

Granada, town of blood. It is a terrible thing for Granada that Lorca died there. It is a terrible thing that somewhere in Granada, perhaps today, there is a man who carries the secret of Lorca's death in his breast. There were, even in my day, such killings in the shadows of the Vermilion Towers, but the excuse had not been found, which served for the murder of Lorca.

It was not his fault that his poems—clear and clean and free from the poison attributed to them—were adopted as battle songs by the enemies of the existing régime; nor did he ever, by written or spoken word, accept his election as a people's leader. It was those very electors who betrayed him to his death—if one accepts the political motive—by binding upon him intentions and motives that are nowhere apparent in his work, save in so far as the passions and sympathies that govern a poet's existence must colour the fruits of his genius.

Again I repeat, that if it was the Fascists who crucified Federico García Lorca, it was the anti-Fascists who played Judas to him. This great poet, this Male Carnation of the soul of Spain, had his roots in no narrow plot of party earth, acrid with enmities. Mirror of the Spanish earth—of its mysticism, its eroticism; deeply infected by the Moorish ethos that breathes in Andalusían dust—it was the tragedy of Lorca that he sang Spain in terms that the disingenuous of both camps could translate to their own advantage; does this not, in itself, prove his universality? It was his tragedy that, writing for intellectuals, the emotional content of his poems, seeping through a rainbow vocabulary, conveyed itself to the great, non-intellectual majority, which, in its simplicity, adapted it to its own idiom of resistance, rebellion and resentment of injustices deep-rooted in the social scheme. That Lorca was conscious of these injustices is visible in every line of his recorded work: that he meant his poems to be used as an incentive to violence between man and man, between party and party is so foreign to the man himself that it is not worth the consideration of any reasonable and unprejudiced person.

There was a strange fatality in Lorca's return to Granada, the home of his youth, there to meet the 'moment of truth' for which his short life and so many of his poems were the preparation. Two years before, in the bullring at Manzanares, had taken place the death of his dear friend, Sanchez Ignacio Mejías, for whom his Lament is among the finest of the many poems of death that Lorca had written; and it seems something more than poetic coincidence that brought death to Mejías in the form of a bull (number 52 of the ganadería of Ayála) named Granadino, and, later, overtook Lorca in the shadow of a Granada wall. Granada, town of blood: whose very name casts a blood-coloured shadow on whom it falls.

> Today as yesterday, my gipsy Death—

wrote his friend Antonio Machado,

> How good it is, to be alone with thee
> In these winds of Granada, of my Granada!

Where else should an Andalusían poet die, than in the town of blood and pomegranates—the town for ever celebrated in his poems and his plays?

Those who, in visiting Granada, ignore Lorca—though they may know each street corner, each staircase, all its markets and madonnas—ignore Granada. Their approach to the gipsies is blind—even blinder than that inevitable to racial antipathy—who have not read *Preciosa and the Wind*, *The Gipsy Nun*, *The Song of the Flogged Gipsy*. Who look at the statue of Mariana Pineda in her little plaza close to the theatre, and have only the guide-book version of her heroism to enlighten them, are indeed in darkness. And who cannot view San Miguel in his alcove through the eyes of Lorca miss altogether the curious, androgynous quality infused by the Granadina into her catholicism.

As the minstrel of Granada, alone, Lorca would not have achieved his high place in the poetic galaxy of his people, and it is in such works as *Yerma* and *Bodas de Sangre* that he lays his hands on immortality, as on the feet of the Crucified; it is in these that he reveals the depths of his tenderness and his closeness to the feminine soul. To read the poems of Lorca in translation is infinitely better than not to know them at all; to see Spain through that curiously coloured vision of his, which, as his friend Gregorio Prieto says, is a painter's vision, is to increase one's awareness of all that normal sight brings within one's range.

Under the shadow of a wall, through a darkness of leaves, passes a ghost whose face is still silver with youth, and his hands filled with the white roses of innocent death. The lament of nightingales for a fellow nightingale falls like tears from the elms, and the towers of the Alhambra veil themselves in everlasting shame.

Duerme, vuela, reposa: Tambien se muere el mar!

CHAPTER XVI

'TO MEET A TORERO'

My friend has come out from England; she is young, blonde and ravishingly pretty, and, having read a few novels with a Spanish background—including my own—her head is all turned with preconceived notions of Spain. On the very first evening, as we sit in swimming suits on the edge of the pool, she confides to me that her one desire in life is to meet a bullfighter.

'Oh Verena! Bullfighters are so boring.'

Indignantly she refers me to my own works.

'Do you call El Bailarín boring?'

I explain, as much as possible in words of one syllable, that El Bailarín is 'literature'; that the *true* bullfighter in my novel, *Matador*, is Bailarinito, and that no one can regard him as an estimable character.

True to her good English breeding, her expensive English boarding school and her 'finishing' in Paris, Verena declares that she can't bear estimable people; that she has come away from England mainly to avoid them, and that she will consider her time wasted unless she meets a really 'typical' bullfighter—whom, incidentally, I restrain her from referring to as a 'toreador.'

'If you wanted to meet *toreros*, you should have gone to Sevilla. Granada is a poor town for the bulls. There's plenty of *afición*—.'

'What's that?' asks Verena, whose reading has evidently not been concentrated.

'Fancy. But the bullring is abominably managed, and they won't pay big money. We've had nothing but a few *novilladas* all the summer.'

157

'But surely you can find me one, *little* bullfighter?' she pleads.

I say sourly that I can find her plenty of 'little' bullfighters: soaking in the taverns, cadging money from anyone weak-minded enough to listen to their hard luck stories, living on cabaret girls, boasting of illusory triumphs, invincibly optimistic about the future, and only prevented (according to themselves) by their misfortune, up to the present, in failing to find a good impresario who will recognize their talents and give them the backing they require, from rivalling Belmonte—or even Joselito.

'You're so cynical!' wails Verena.

'If you care to lift your eyes,' I add, 'you may see a specimen of the breed, plastered on the wall at the top of the garden, where he has been trying to attract our attention for the last three-quarters of an hour.'

'Is *that* a bullfighter?'—She is obviously crestfallen. 'It's not a bit like one. Are you sure?'

'Quite sure. What are you looking for?—the *coleta?* They're made of horsehair and they pin them on for the fight,' I say unkindly. 'José de La Zubia had two fights last year, in somebody's *cuadrilla*, somewhere out in the country; he missed with all his darts and he's lost his reputation. He's probably hanging round for the remains of that stew we had for lunch; he's some sort of relation of Rosario's, and she gives him the odds and ends.'

Verena is shaken. But during supper, to which Frasquito is bidden, she returns to the subject. I translate for Frasquito's benefit.

'Verena wants to meet a bullfighter.'

Frasquito smiles finely, lowers his eyelids, and obviously dismisses this as only another instance of British eccentricity.

'There's Luis . . .' I have realized that, sooner or later something will have to be done about it.

Frasquito indicates that it is quite out of the question.

'*Es muy mal educado.*'

'Good heavens, I don't want an educated bullfighter! I don't suppose they go to the universities!'

I explain mildly that *educado* refers to good manners, not to intellectual equipment, and that it is not unusual for bull-fighters—at all events in the higher ranks—to have both. I cite Belmonte's *aficion* for literature and painting. Verena sulks. I reflect uncomfortably upon her father, the bishop, upon her aunt in-waiting, upon her brothers in the smarter regiments and her innumerable county connections. I am (ostensibly) responsible for Verena in Granada, and it looks as if I am in for trouble.

'Why can't you ask this Luis—whatever to supper?' pouts Verena—a proposition which would blanch Frasquito if he understood it.

I explain that, while it would be an honour, as well as a pleasure, to ask certain bullfighters to supper, I have no intention of inviting the riff-raff of the ring to make free of the villa.

'If you want to cultivate bullfighters,' I tell her with asperity, 'you'd better go to Sevilla at *feria* time, and imitate some of your compatriots, who sit about the lounge of the Cristina in fake gipsy clothes, to amuse the Spaniards.'

Verena whines that she wants to meet a bullfighter.

Eventually, one evening, under the trees outside the café de la Alameda, we contact Luis.

He happens, this evening, to be looking prosperous. Having won a lottery, he has pacified his tailor, got a new suit out of him, a handful of pesetas in his pocket, and has collected a bunch of flashy young Granadinos who like to be seen around in the company of a bullfighter. I recognize that, from a foreigner's point of view, Luis represents the *beau ideal* of the bullfighter; tall, handsome in a dissipated fashion, with the nervous slouch which is à la mode among smart young men—in London no less than in Granada.

'Oh—who's that wonderful-looking person?'

'There's your bullfighter.—*Muy buenas*, Luis.'

Luis, who, as Frasquito says, has no manners, says '*Olá*,' and stares very hard at Verena, who is wearing rather more jewellery than usual, and, suffering from a rush of Spain to the head, has copied my housemaid in thrusting a rose into her blonde hair. Murmurs of '*la rubia*' and '*guapa*' from the flashy young men in no way discompose her; she is all dewy-eyed at meeting her first bullfighter. Stifled by the perfume of *Tabu* which Luis and his companions scatter over our table, I accept, however, the inevitable, and invite them to sit down and take a *copita* with us. Which they do—Luis with an air of conferring an immense favour. Verena immediately begs me to ask him where he is fighting next, and he mentions a town of so little prestige that no one has ever heard of it. Verena beams as graciously as if he had said the Monumentale at Madrid.

'And how many fights has he got this season?'

'He says he is booked for seventeen *corridas*. He is a b-liar,' I inform her, with the freedom which speaking English confers upon the stranger in Granada.

'I've always died to meet a matador,' sighs Verena.

'Don't be cuckoo. He's a *banderillero*, and a rotten one at that.' I say this with so flattering a smile upon Luis that he is convinced I am paying him the greatest possible compliments, and his expression becomes fatuous. Out of the corner of his eye I see him valuing the diamond that pins Verena's silk scarf.

Frasquito passes, with a couple of stately Granadino gentlemen; his bow is so distant that it is as if the *sierra* inclined its icy head. I realize that this public hobnobbing with Luis and his gang is going to take some living down.

Deciding that the diamond brooch and a pair of Tiffany bracelets entitle her to his attentions, Luis pays Verena a couple of raw compliments, which I emasculate in the translation.

'Tell him I'd adore to see him in his fighting clothes!'

Luis preens himself; the satellites are now fascinated with Verena, who, looking lovely, is unaware of their existence.

'You can tell the señorita I will put them on for her, if she likes,' he condescendingly informs me.

'Oh—will he *really*? And has he got any photographs of himself?'

Luis has distributed all his photographs; he is intending, however, to have some done, immediately. The señorita is *encantada*. I order, *faute de mieux*, another round of drinks. The cold eye of Frasquito penetrates me, from his adjacent table, and I shrug my shoulders.

Luis and Verena, neither of whom can speak a syllable of the other's language, are now, clearly, 'on terms'. The satellites—one of whom, it turns out, knows a few words of English—as in honour bound, are playing up admirably; with a shrewd eye on the situation, Luis is promoted to the rank of matador, having received the *alternativa* only a few weeks ago. (Verena's eye seeks mine reproachfully) Luis smiles uneasily, and gives me furtive glances, hoping I will not let him down. Carried away by their own eloquence, his friends describe how, at his last fight (they don't know that I know all about that disgraceful affair at Jérez de Marquesada) he was given the ears and tail, and that he is booked for Madrid in July, with Lalanda and Ortega. One of the party questions me rapidly, on the length of Verena's stay in Granada, and whether she is *casada*. I say firmly that her parents have permitted her to make a short stay with me, before joining her family and her *novio* (why, after all, should fiction be confined to the satellites?) in Palma de Mallorca.

Verena turns to me radiantly.

'Luis wants to take us for a drive in the country.'

'*What?*'

'Oh, darling, look what a lovely night it is! *Don't* be stuffy. I suppose you wouldn't let me go by myself.'

'I should think not! And I'm not going to scandalize Granada by careering round the *sierras* with Luis and his friends.'

This precipitates a crisis. Verena is in active rebellion, and Luis is piqued by my evident opposition into partisan-ship with her. I try desperately to catch Frasquito's eye, but he has washed his hands of us. He is deep in conversation with the people at his own table.

Eventually I agree—not to go for a drive, but to join Luis and his friends up at Luisa's tavern for an hour. To stop argument, I hail a taxi, push Verena into it, and, giving the driver rapid instructions, am off before the others have time to get in.

'But what are you doing——?'

'If they want to come, they know the way.'

'I hadn't any idea you were so conventional!'—She sounds disappointed.

'I'm not; but I happen to live in Granada, and I don't see any point in setting people's hair on end for the sake of an evening with Luis's gang!'

Privately, I have hopes that we have shaken them off, but I have under-rated the power of Tiffany. We have not been sitting in the *patio* more than twenty minutes when the party arrives: augmented by two gipsy girls, unknown to me personally, and some guitarristas. In a moment the table is covered with bottles of La Riva wine, the *piropo* is in full swing. Somebody buys Verena a jasmine snowball, somebody else buys her almonds. I watch with a kind of sadness her radiant response to the attention she receives; it is like a child at a party . . . I remember an old nursery saying: 'This will all end in a good cry!'

The gipsies dance; having had a great deal too much sherry, Verena stands up too, and dances with Luis, to wild applause. She is in heaven; she is dancing with a real bull-fighter. Luisa tells me I have 'the black face', and asks what is the matter. I cannot explain; Luisa, like all the tavern keepers, is delighted to entertain a bullfighter—particularly when there is a reasonable prospect of getting her bill paid. Looking on me as security for this, she glitters with affability and brings more and more bottles of La Riva.

A definitely hazy Verena confides to me, on the way home, that she has a date with Luis at the photographer's on the following morning.

'But he's *lovely*? How can you say he's *mal educado?*— I've never had such a wonderful night in my life!'

We are in the town at an early hour—in a jeweller's shop in the Zácatin. Luis—bless his romantic heart—has confided his wish to have some souvenir of the señorita. I suggest a holy medal—and hastily add that it need not be a gold one. Verena is doubtful.

'He was mad on this pin of mine. I suppose it isn't done to give men jewellery?'

I am very firm on the point. We go up to the photographer's in the Alhambra; the appointment having been for half-past ten, it is a quarter to twelve when Luis saunters in, followed by a shabby individual carrying a large bundle done up in a checked table cloth, which turns out to be the fighting suit.

We simmer in the studio, which, with its glass roof, is like a grill at this hour of the morning, while Luis arrays himself.

When at last he emerges, I get a faint glimmer of the fascination which the bullfighter holds for the unsophisticated foreigner. Luis is one of the few tall bullfighters; usually they are short, even mean-looking. His height is that of Villalta, his proportions much finer, without the ridiculous long neck and sloping shoulders which gained the 'Aragonese telegraph pole' his nickname. Not yet having started the day's drinking, his nervous tic is in abeyance, and as he comes out into the sun—from which he winces—he is impressive enough to quicken a heart much more sophisticated than Verena's. Mentally I curse Luis, his good looks and his ridiculous fighting suit, which is cheap and showy: a magenta silk which could hardly be more unfortunate for his sallow complexion. I notice that he has borrowed, or stolen, a long matador's cape, in place of the short one to which he is entitled; this is very beautiful, with the Virgen de Pilar embroidered in gold tinsel on a ground of violet.

His eyeballs are as yellow as guineas, his face grey and furrowed like a man of forty, although, according to his record, he cannot be much more than twenty-seven or eight. He is in rotten condition: thigh muscles so shrunken that the silk of his breeches, which should grip them like the casing of a sausage, bags away—a nice invitation for the bull, if he happened to be going into the ring. But the violet, the magenta and the black sash—into which he spins himself with Verena holding the other end—compose beautifully; with the *coleta* pinned in place, and the *montera* tilted over his eyes, Luis is enjoying one of those few moments of pure satisfaction that a bullfighter can know, when he gets into the terrible beauty of his clothes for the ring. Death is not at his elbow there is no horror ahead of him, and he basks in the admiration of a lovely—and rich—young girl.

'Tell him he looks divine!'

Although I moderate this in the translation, Verena's eyes defeat my discretion, and over Luis's face slips the thin mask of insufferable vanity that he wears at the height of success—either with bulls or women.

The medal is presented, and Luis has just enough 'educacion' to conceal his disappointment. I am sure he had hoped, at the least, for a gold cigarette case, or for a pair of jewelled cuff-links in the same class as Verena's brooch! It is weak-minded of me, perhaps, to be sorry for him; it is always easier to contribute to a person's self-illusion than to shatter it. The great matadores get diamonds, emeralds, even motor-cars from their foreign admirers. Poor Luis! How should he understand the sentiment which invest this gift, of a little holy medal, from an English girl of nineteen?

Now a curious thing takes place. The camera is run into position, and the subject is invited to take his stand against a backcloth representing a section of the Alhambra. And for some reason all the glory departs from Luis. His skin goes powdery, he moistens his lips, his eyes protrude with horror. Suddenly I am reminded of something: women in the souks of Morocco, when one tries to take a photograph of them. It is an act of ill-omen; with the transference of the image to the film in the camera, the soul of the subject likewise passes from her—such, at least, is the belief; only the more hardened will remain, exposed to the menacing little eye of the camera; the more modest, or the simpler, flee in terror, covering their faces. I wonder how much Moorish blood is in Luis, as his shoulders hunch themselves, his fingers grip tremblingly on the folds of the borrowed cape, and his eyes, fixed on the camera, take on the same blank stare of petrifaction with which he faces his bulls. Cringing, unwilling, one feels sure that, if the *barrera* were handy, he would leap over it; he stands revealed for what he is—a frightened braggart, who never in his life placed an honest dart, or trailed a cape, unless he had made sure of his margin of safety.

Sorry for Verena, I turn towards her—only to discover that love is blind.

'Isn't he wonderful?—I wish he'd lift his head just a little bit more. I wonder how we'll be posed for the one together?'

It is the first I have heard of a photograph *au pair*, but comfort myself temporarily with the thought that, if Luis goes on this way, he will probably collapse in a swoon at our feet before his own 'positions' are finished. Unfortunately, he appears to gain a little confidence as the sitting proceeds, and the last two poses are slightly better than the earlier ones.

The photographer now has an inspiration, and drags forward a piece of cardboard wall, on which Verena is invited to sit, while Luis is supposed to stand behind it, in a romantic attitude which, however, he fails to achieve. It is left for my poor Verena to do the romance: gazing upward with liquid eyes of adoration, while Luis, standing like a block of wood, looks shifty.

'I say, how soon will they be ready?' Verena asks eagerly. 'I must have one to send Aunt Phyllis for her birthday.'

I refrain from pointing out that I see no excuse for ruining Aunt Phyllis's birthday, and Luis slouches off to get out of his clothes. Before he goes, I do the polite thing by inviting him to take a glass of wine with us in the Casa de Apolonio, but he says sulkily that he has friends waiting for him in the town, shakes hands limply, and disappears. *Claro:* if one wastes one's morning dressing up for the benefit of an eccentric *inglesa*, one expects to get something more out of it than a five duro medal. Verena is thoughtful as we stroll back to the villa.

'Do you think he's cross about something?—He was much nicer last night.'

I explain kindly that all artists are temperamental, and that Luis may be suffering from an attack of indigestion, which is one of the bullfighters' several occupational diseases. Verena reproaches me with my materialistic view, then brightens as she suggests that if we go down to the Alameda again tonight, we may meet Luis.

'And I'm learning quite a lot of Spanish!—I always say that's the only way to learn a foreign language—to talk it with somebody you're interested in.'

I grasp that I am going to have to keep quite an eye on my Verena for the remainder of her stay.

The photographs arrive: the black and white truth, at which Verena gazes speechlessly.

'But . . . it isn't even *like* him!'

There is one photograph of Luis, signed, '*A la simpatica señorita Verena, su amigo Luis Calva de Granada,*' and there are six of the *au pair*.

'But he hasn't even kept one of us for himself!—I don't blame him,' says Verena valiantly, turning away so that I shall not see her tearful eyes. 'I look awful—like one of those common wax figures in Oxford Street—I think it's a beastly photographer!'

It is, perhaps, unkind of me to lay before her the enclosed bill—the photographs have been sent direct from the shop— for six cabinet photographs of the señorita with the torero Luis Calvo de Granada, and two hundred and fifty of the single figure: which she tears from me, saying that indeed she won't have that!—and it is unfortunate that Luisa happens to call in, and, in the course of conversation, to mention that the account for our evening at the tavern amounts to four hundred and eighty-two pesetas—'The gipsies, as you know, are expensive, and there were three guitarristas; and naturally the señores were drinking the best wine . . .'

'But I thought it was Luis's party,' Verena is näive enough to remark, when I pass this information on to her.

I explain tenderly that no party including Luis is ever Luis's party, but that, on the whole, I feel we have paid cheaply for her *béguin*.

We see nothing more of Luis during the remainder of Verena's visit, and, among the debris of her departure, I am interested to observe the torn pieces of a sheaf of photographs. I heave a deep breath of relief, not having had the heart to tell her that, passing the photographer's one morning, an assistant ran out to give me the little medal, which Luis had left, forgotten, on the dressing-room floor.

CHAPTER XVII

THE WITCH

THERE was once a very agreeable young Spanish nobleman, whose name runs into so many syllables and is complicated by so many conjunctives that I have not the heart to inflict it upon English readers, so let us call him simply Don Guzmán, which imposes no strain, either upon the memory or the pronunciation. Like a good many young men in his position he was extremely plagued by his mother to whom he was devoted, and who had, in accordance with the custom of the times, picked out a wife for him.

Now it is notorious that mothers and sons rarely see eye to eye when it comes to this matter of betrothal, so no one will be surprised to hear that Don Guzmán did not so much dislike the wife his mother had chosen for him, as he was bored stiff by her. She was a pattern of all the virtues, had never since childhood spoken to man other than her own father, was as plump as a pigeon and carried a dowry which would enable Don Guzmán to indulge to the full all his favourite and expensive pastimes, such as horsebreeding, hunting and falconry.

So he was fain to make the best of the situation, for young women of fortune, virtue and passable good looks were not to be found in quantity in his town, and were in fact so rare throughout the province that the mothers of marriageable young men fought like wild cats to secure the best prizes for their sons.

Doña Vespasiana, who was Don Guzmán's mother, had won the battle by force of the biggest vocabulary, the most formidable personality and the strongest determination among the competitors: backed by the fact that her late husband's family was much the most distinguished in the town.

Now it so happened that this town in which Don Guzmán lived was very much plagued by witches, for this was the Middle Ages, and witches were one of the most tiresome and troublesome problems that the local administrations of the period had to tackle. And what with the tempests that raged nightly against the ramparts (which all who lived in that quarter agreed were caused by the whirl of the broomsticks upon which these unwelcome visitors travelled), and what with the peculiar things that kept occurring to horses and cattle (there was a horse belonging to the tallow chandler, whose head had swollen to three times its natural size, and a cow had recently given birth to a calf with five legs), not to mention the very much hushed-up affair of the alcalde's daughter, who, it was whispered, had had a baby so like a little brown pig, it was a mercy it died—people were beginning to feel that it was high time something was done about these witches. But nobody was very keen on tackling the matter, because witch-hunting was not regarded as a healthy form of sport, and the young men of the town, although not lacking in ordinary valour, drew the line— very properly—at the supernatural.

It happened, however, that the new Bishop was a man very zealous in the persecution of witches. He was not a particularly godly man, but what he lacked in spiritual direction he made up for by his appreciation and love of good wine, which he spoke of and preached about as God's greatest blessing to mankind: a doctrine which recommended him very warmly to his parishioners; and by the fertility he displayed in devising torments for any persons suspected of possessing the attributes of witches. Hearing from afar of the reputation of Don Guzmán's town for witch-hauntings, he had applied for its bishopric, and, on securing the advancement, had rubbed his hands with glee at the prospect of revelling in his favourite sport.

Having met Don Guzmán, he decided that this was a young man of no ordinary valour, and hearing that he was shortly to be married, he sent for him to the palace. Having paid him the compliment (which a young man appreciates) of dining him well, the Bishop proceeded to tell him, in confidence, the story of the alcalde's daughter. Don Guzmán expressed a suitable horror, remarking that it was quite time someone took these witches seriously; whereupon the Bishop remarked, Yes, indeed, if they carried their tricks so far as to bedevil the daughter of one of the town's most illustrious citizens, there was no knowing where they would finish. Don Guzmán, staring hypnotized into the eyes of the Bishop, understood, as he was intended to do, that, in his Lordship's opinion, if the witches were allowed to get away with their latest prank, it was at least on the cards that the wife of Don Guzmán might, when her time came, be the victim of their misplaced sense of humour.

That night Don Guzmán said to his mother, 'I have a good mind to look into this witch business myself. It is high time someone took it in hand.' With this suggestion his mother was in full agreement: for, apart from being an intrepid woman, she also knew the full story of the alcalde's daughter, and it had occurred to her that, not to put too fine a point on it, it would be a nice thing if she was presented with a pig for a grandchild!

So, to cut a long story short, it was decided that Don Guzmán should lead an expedition to that highest peak of the mountains which so long as anyone can remember has been called Silla de las Brujas—the Witches' Chair; and that the Bishop should accompany him, and that they should take with them eight men, picked for their sturdy scepticism and lack of imagination, and a captain of the military guard, to bind the witches and bring them down to the town to be burnt: the presence of the Bishop to be accepted by all as security for the personal safety of the expedition, for the witches would surely be powerless against the holy influences at his disposal.

So in the early dawn of a winter's morning they set forth, in this order: first rode Don Guzmán, upon his Arab stallion, wearing round his neck the special holy medals which his mother had had blessed by the Pope, and had kept in reserve for some such emergency as this. His rich cloak of padded cloth and fur, crusted with embroideries, protected his body, as his gloves of fur and steel were protection to his hands. He carried a sword of the best Toledo steel, and two pistols, loaded in readiness, hung at his saddle bow. At his elbow rode the Bishop, also swaddled in furs, upon a wicked-looking black mule, sixteen hands high, that knew by instinct every pebble of the mountain paths; and in their wake, upon a variety of indifferent hacks, came the eight picked men of the guard, with their captain in charge.

As they rode out of the town, many hands were waved from lighted balconies, and there was a noise of women's weeping; but Doña Vespasiana, who was too brave, and Doña Caridad, who was too foolish to weep—though no doubt both would have done so, could they have foreseen the outcome of the day—cheered Don Guzmán with smiles, as he rode beneath their *rejas*.

It was obvious that the witches had seen the expedition starting, for the cavalcade had barely reached the mountains when they drew down upon the Silla de Las Brujas a dense volume of cloud, that broke into swirling eddies down the clefts of the mountain side. The Bishop rose in his stirrups and made a large sign of the cross, but it was agreed that they were at too great a distance for this to take effect, and, lowering their heads against the piercing wind that blew out of the gullies, they moved upward, the road thinning gradually to a mere frayed ribbon that looped the chasmic heights and depths of the ravines. Every now and then they were obliged to take refuge from the wind's savagery in the cave-like recesses scooped by the rain out of the rocks, and whenever they did so, the Bishop entertained them, and raised their laugher and anticipation with stories of the witch-baitings he had organized in the past.

It was when they were emerging from one of these shelters that they heard above them a hollow thunder, and, looking upwards, saw a great boulder, which had loosened itself from the rock face, come crashing downwards. Each man set spurs to his horse, but the path was so narrow that only one could move forward at a time, and the rock,

descending, caught and crushed out of existence the last
man in the line: an incident which, as may well be imagined,
cast a great shadow upon the party, and particularly upon the
man who had ridden immediately ahead of the victim, for
the dead man was his brother.

Don Guzmán and the Bishop exchanged glances, and the
latter was delivered of a very unpriestly oath. Neither was
unduly nervous, Don Guzmán trusting in his medals, and
the Bishop in the holiness of his office, which naturally
protected him from witch-malice. But the rest of the party
had got the jumps, and communicated them to their horses,
which started to prance and teeter in a fashion extremely
dangerous to the whole expedition, upon a path hardly wider
than the top of a stone wall. And coming suddenly round a
sharp corner upon a cactus, whose trunk had a certain
devilish resemblance to the human form, one of the horses
reared.

There was a moment of sickening uncertainty, while he
and his rider swayed upon the brink of the abyss, and then,
almost noiselessly, the pair of them vanished—and seconds
went by before the others heard the crash below, that told
them the rocks had claimed two more victims.

Purple with rage, the Bishop again made the sign of the
cross, and spoke an invocation at which he fully expected
the cactus to vanish: but it remained there, crooked like a
beckoning finger over the depth of the ravine, so that they
were all obliged to admit that it was simply a cactus, and not
a witch in disguise.

There was now about them such a silence that the
blood of each man drummed in his ears. The rocks were
iron-coloured, and the path like iron to the feet; the cold
was formidable, for they were getting near the snowline.

For Don Guzmán and the Bishop, both well-nourished
and nicely snuggled in their furs, this state of affairs was
not so painful; but for the soldiers of the guard, indifferently
nourished on garrison food and protected only by their
leather jackets, it was a different matter. For the cold, as
they went on, seemed to take on a quality of personal enmity:
it had in it some horrible element, something tactile, that

slid into each man's clothing, down the back of his neck, through the latchets of his jacket, where it seemed to turn into icy fingers that pinched a man's breast and drove themselves in shafts of pain into his heart.

Great as was their fortitude, the six remaining soldiers who followed their captain had all they could do to stifle their groans as they went on into the teeth of the wind: and teeth, in this case, mind you, is no mere figure of speech, for, from Don Guzmán to the meanest soldier, there was none who did not feel the wind's attack like fangs, tearing at his nose and ears, and blinding his eyes with stinging moisture.

'This is the very devil,' muttered Don Guzmán, as his horse stumbled in rounding another perilous bend. Even the Bishop's zest was a little abated; nothing of him was visible except his two angry eyes, between the brim of his beaver hat and the high, fur-trimmed collar of his robe; and during the last kilometro he had invented two separate and distinct tortures for witches, of so sanguinary a nature that, for the credit of the Church, one must refrain from describing here. To his honour let it be said, however, that it was he who took the lead when, at a point where the path was all but broken away, where the cavalcade resembled nothing so much as flies clinging to the sheer rock face, and there was a bare hand's breadth between each man and eternity, a cloud swept down and engulfed them, so that each man appeared to his companions like a fluctuating pillar of the mist. It was the Bishop then who, thrusting past Don Guzmán, cried that his mule would not fail them, and was the first to be swallowed in the wreathing brume.

As for the other horses, poor brutes!—their sides were red with the spurs their riders were forced to employ to drive them along this parapct of death. Nor was their only horror the cloud, for in the heart of the cloud, and seemingly all about them, was a noise like the beating of wings, as though they were disturbing an eagle's eyrie, and each man feared at any moment to be swept from his horse's back by the rush of the great birds. Yet they followed where the Bishop's voice could be heard roaring a psalm, and at the end of a time that seemed to them for ever, they came out on the farther side of the cloud which, when they looked back upon it, was coloured like sulphur, and clung like a gigantic caul to the rock face. So they knew the witches had made another attack, and that they had been saved only through the sanctity of his Lordship; and as they happened to have reached a little plateau, where there was room for them to cluster together, each man descended from his horse, save the Bishop and Don Guzmán, and, kneeling tremblingly, besought the Bishop to lay his blessing upon each one of them, for his individual protection. When they rose to their feet, the captain of the guard looking upon his men saw that they were only four.

Suddenly now the path, whose rise so far had been gradual, tilted precipitously upwards, and they knew they were upon the last stage of their ascent. A little farther, and they would be obliged to abandon their horses, for the topmost pinnacles of the Silla de la Brujas is scalable only on hands and knees, and that only if a man has a steady head and a heart without fear. And, without a moment's warning, the winter sun shone out, and smote into their eyes like a scimitar of gold, so that they had to clap their hands before their eyes to avoid blindness; for the snows lay before them, with their murderous glitter, and the near escarpments, in their glassy drapery of icicles, caught the sunlight and turned it upon them like a thousand facets of mirror glass.

'These are good witches,' murmured Don Guzmán, unable to withhold admiration from such evidence of pure artistry: adding hastily, so that the Bishop should not mistake his meaning 'Good, I mean, in the sense that their invention is indefatigable'.

The Bishop growled and his expression was bloodthirsty. He even ran his tongue along his lips in anticipation of the spectacle his invention provided for him: of the witchburning in the market-place, while the dancing people crowded his palace steps and extolled his fame as a witch-baiter and the saviour of their fortunes. But Don Guzmán, turning his back for a moment on the glare of the sun, saw an ugly sight; for one poor fellow, the brother of him who first had died, seized with vertigo, and maddened by the fearful experiences through which he had passed, gave a scream and, driving his spurs into his horse, sent it leaping outwards. Horror-stricken, the whole party watched man and horse toppling, toppling, in a series of flashes as the sun's rays caught the accoutrements, until the valley fog received them; and so great was the distance they fell that not a sound came to the listeners upon the heights.

Brave as he was, Don Guzmán faltered. He began to wonder if the destruction of witches was worth such a sacrifice of gallant lives. But a most unholy passion had entered into the Bishop, who, saying no word, but setting his lips in a thin line, struck his mule and urged it upwards. And now, though they were, to the visible eye, but five, there rode at each man's elbow an invisible companion, a wan horseman whose black eye-sockets and bared jaws materialized each rider's fear and jostled him closer to the unspeakable brink.

They were now among the very summits of the mountains, and as far as the eye could see, these pricked the sky with points of frosted iron. Their pale sides rushed down into unimaginable crevasses, and a restlessness of light lay over the whole scene, very deceptive to the eye; for the clouds, blown by the bitter gale, resembled the curling smoke of a great bonfire, through which came and went the fickle sunlight. Immediately above their heads towered the dread peaks of the Silla itself, like a rotten, three-fanged tooth, pierced by the black mouth of a cavern.

It was the Bishop who insisted, when they dismounted from their horses, upon calling a halt for food. They had been riding for many hours, and each was weak for lack of sustenance; but to the rest it seemed an insane tempting of Providence, to sit down and eat within the very sight of witches. The food itself might be bedevilled, and turn to poison in their mouths. But the Bishop's stomach, so tenderly nurtured, was plaguing him, and he had, moreover, a saddlebag of delicious provender, including a young turkey stuffed with chestnuts and two bottles of his best wine, which he set forth and proceeded to enjoy, untroubled by the fact that the soldiers had nothing better than bread and garlic sausage with which to stay their equal hunger.

So they all sat down, each man with his fear beside him, and, hungry as they were, the food stuck in their gullets. The soldiers kept their heads tucked down, so as not to see the black shapes in the sky, which each man believed to be the witches themselves, although Don Guzmán, looking gloomily but steadfastly upon them, knew them to be eagles, and wondered how long it would be before their vile appetites were appeased.

There was not a sound to be heard, save the Bishop, smacking his lips as the wine ran down into his belly. Finding their sun-magic of no avail, the witches had evidently decided to change their tactics, for blackness now started to heap itself in the sky, and a screaming scud of gale, rising without warning, nipped up one of the empty saddle bags and launched it like a leaf upon the air: which each man took as a personal warning of his own most probable fate.

And as the darkness grew thicker, it became like a sombre canvas, upon which each man painted his longing for the safety of home: and such a host of little children, of tall boys and pretty girls, of women's breasts and arms shone pale upon the dark background of the sky that these lonely artists sat petrified by the extent of their own achievement, while the tears ran into the stubble of their chins, and their lips shook before the vision of all they had renounced for their city's sake. And of all the witches' magic this surely was the strangest and most potent, for it drew the very hearts out of their victims' breasts, so that not one of them would have gone a step further, even at the bidding of Don Guzmán, had not the Bishop, seeing well which way the wind was blowing, very reluctantly sacrificed his second bottle of wine in order to put the remaining men and their captain in a mood for continuing on their way.

However, as they had all had very little to eat, the wine, which was very potent, mounted quickly to their heads. Their valour presently became excessive, and, without waiting for the direction of their leaders, they rushed upon the upward clamber, which was the last stage of their journey. No longer were they haunted by the pale fear-spectres which had ridden beside them on their perilous path, for all around them, beckoning and waving, floated in air the visions of their many and tender loves, while the thin ice-glazing of the rocks slid beneath their feet and hands, and first one, and then another, lost hold, and departed on the bosom of a dream for the infinite bliss each one had pictured.

When Don Guzmán and the Bishop, both grievously short of breath, faced each other upon a ledge immediately below the mouth of the cavern, they were alone. There were tears in Don Guzmán's eyes, but nothing save a vicious triumph in those of the Bishop; and Don Guzmán, who would fain have dedicated a prayer to the souls of the lost ones, and who was not above putting up a last supplication to Heaven on his own account, was defeated in both of his intentions by the action of the Bishop, who, standing upright, and flinging out his arms so that the whole of his body made the sign of the cross, cried in a loud voice upon the Devil's emissaries to declare themselves.

At first there was no reply. The Bishop's cape cracked like a banner in the gale, as his stout figure braced itself on wide-planted feet to resist the wind's attack. Upon his broad bosom smouldered a cross of rubies and emeralds, at whose heart lay a relic warranted to repel every assault of the powers of evil; but in the strange light and darkness that lay upon the Silla the very cross seemed to alter its nature, and to become a symbol of evil rather than of good.

The Bishop repeated his invocation, adding to it a denunciation of the infernal crafts that had resisted their ascent; and just as the last thunders of his voice were dying against the clanging gong of the sky, there appeared in the mouth of the cave the small, neat head of a woman, prim, bird-like, and no more discomposing than that of the modest young housewife who leans from her balcony to take her morning roll from the baker's basket. She had a full, pleasant bosom, which she pressed against her folded arms as she leaned upon the rock ledge, to look calmly down upon her visitors.

Now, it is a disconcerting thing, when one looks for elf-locks, the dribble of toothless jaws and all the ugly panoply of vice, to come upon a perfectly modest, discreet-looking young person whose presence at the Mass would rouse no unseemly degree of attention among her neighbours; and thus, for a moment, the witch appeared, to the surprise of the Bishop—which, however, he quickly conquered—and the confusion of Don Guzmán.

The latter's instinct, as he obeyed the Bishop's exhortation to follow him, was to sweep off his hat, and apologize in the politest possible manner for the intrusion, when he saw, to his horror, the Bishop proceeding to unknot the cord from his waist, and heard him calling upon the young woman in a peremptory voice to come and be bound. It was only then that Don Guzmán realized two things: the first, that he stood, for the first time in his life, in the presence of a witch, and, second, that his emotions were stirred as they had never been in any of his dealings with the lady who expected, shortly, to become his wife. The two reflections gave him a coldness about the roots of his hair, and it was with resentment, mingled with an enormous misgiving, that he saw the Bishop, presumably in self-protection, raise the great square cross at arm's length between him and the witch: an act which may have been prudent, but which seriously hampered him in his struggles with his waistcord.

'*Caramba*,' said the witch mildly. 'That's a pretty thing!'

And Don Guzmán, watching her widening eyes, was stunned to see the colours of the cross reflected in them, so that they appeared all striped with green and crimson between their fringes of blackest silk. Enormous grew her eyes, and in each was a small square cross of red and green, that grew as the pupils dilated. And Don Guzmán realized that the cross had done its work in uncovering her diabolical quality.

'*Caramba*,' she remarked again. 'I would like to have that to wear.' And, as though further to increase the unease of her audience, the witch began to laugh, and this, and the red and green crosses in her eyes, completed their appalled recognition of her unholy entity, for there was that in her laughter

only to be accounted for by the possession of powers unknown to the Bishop and his attendant hierography.

'Come: help me to bind her!' grated the Bishop between
his clenched teeth. There was about him so little that was
holy, as he advanced upon the witch, that Don Guzmán's
soul revolted once and for all against the Church and the
cruelty it authorized. The Bishop, whom, a few moments
ago, he had regarded as a fine fellow, zealous for the right
and full of heroism, suddenly appeared to him in the light of
a meddlesome bully, whom it would be pleasant to see
meeting his deserts. Becoming conscious of his change of
opinion, Don Guzmán started violently, for this could be
nothing less than the utmost subtlety of witchcraft.

He saw the pair of them standing, so close they were
almost breast to breast, and the encounter of their eyes was
like the bared blades of swords. And he saw that, although
the Bishop held the cross in his hands, the infernal crosses
that burned in the witch's eyes outshone the holy symbol and
reduced its fires to a lifeless dullness. And while Don
Guzmán watched, he saw her reach out her hand and, quietly
taking the cross from the Bishop's, lay it upon her own
breast, where, in some miraculous fashion, it burst into a
flame of ruby and emerald.

'It's a pretty thing,' repeated the witch reflectively, and
fingered it with childlike satisfaction, smiling into the
Bishop's face, as he stood petrified by the enormity of her
act. 'But it is I, not you, who become it the better!'

And, whether it was Don Guzmán's imagination, or
whether it was the antic sun that caught the jewels of the
cross, but its rays seemed to grow and lengthen until the
young woman stood in a penumbra of red and green, of thin,
shivering lines of diabolical light that broke from the
symbol on her bosom.

Driven to insanity by this act of sacrilege, the Bishop,
raving, thrust his hand into the folds of his robe, which, as
Don Guzmán knew, concealed the weapons he always
carried: the pistols whose consecrated bullets were said to
be proof against the Devil himself. In other circumstances
nothing would have induced him to make use of them, for by

doing so he cheated himself of the exquisite climax to his favourite adventure—the public torture of his victim, to which, through long practice, he had added so many refinements. But the sight of the cross blazing upon the witch's breast, and her general air of lightness and mockery, had driven him mad, and he found himself unable to wait for his consummation.

As Don Guzmán stood paralysed, and while the witch smiled, almost foolishly, into the Bishop's face, making no movement of fear or self-protection, there was driven into the mind of Don Guzmán, with the force with which a nail is driven into a board, a thought so evil that none but the witch—who had not, so far, paid him the smallest overt attention—could have set it there; and automatically obeying his thought, he whipped his sword from its scabbard and silently, without warning, he ran the Bishop through from behind.

He let the blade sag, and his wrist crack, as the heavy body doubled upon the steel, and only when the Bishop lay dead at his feet did Don Guzmán realize that, driven by some occult force beyond the limits of his own volition, he had committed, in cold blood, a murder for which, for sure, his soul would go to hell. He had, by his own act, deprived himself of the only human society that remained to him in his strange adventure, and now stood, defenceless and companionless, before those powers of evil he had pledged himself to destroy.

As he stood, appalled by his own action—for Don Guzmán was a good young man and had no villainy in him, although less fuss was made in those days than in our own about the taking of human life—and almost forgetful of the witch, who had made no sound or sign during these proceedings, she moved quietly to his side and took his hand in hers; and as palm touched palm, he felt her spell upon him, so that he could neither move nor speak, save by her clemency. And he understood that it was she who had made him do this thing, although, surely, she could have found defences of her own against the threatened assault. And because she had deliberately made him the instrument of this fearful crime, he could feel himself committed to her for evermore: a feeling which filled himself with an intoxication of excitement and terror.

And thus they stood, higher than human thought, more solitary than the human soil in its moment of escape from the body, with the mountains beneath them and space on every side, until she drew him after her into the cavern.

Now indeed Don Guzmán, whose senses were already reeling, received another shock; for the place was scrupulously clean and neat, with cooking-pots and household implements in admirable order and a good deal of whitewash splashed about, with a homely effect that suggested that, witch though she might be, the young woman had domestic instincts. There was even a canary in its cage, and a row of pot-plants, although these were not of the kind one meets with commonly upon the town balconies.

'I like housekeeping,' the witch said carelessly, as though he had spoken his thoughts aloud; and again, as she turned towards him, he felt, pouring over him, so delicious a sorcery that he had no desire save to surrender himself to it completely—although, by such a surrender, he knew he was betraying his town, its people, his mother, and Caridad, who was waiting to marry him. None of which things, as he was aware, would form substance for much of an argument with the witch, were he to advance them to her.

Nevertheless, so overwhelming was the effect that she had upon him that, gradually reassured by her apparent complaisance and more and more overcome, by the rush of emotion she caused in him, he started to give practical expression to it . . .

'We shall have many children,' the witch declared, some hours later.

She had lighted a little lamp and closed the entrance to the cavern with a curtain of heavy leather; the cross upon her breast had shrunk to its original dimensions and appeared no more than a very pretty ornament for a pretty young woman; because, as in the case of any ordinary girl, her looks were very much improved by being made love to.

'We shall found a city of our own, and our children shall

build it. In the morning I shall show you where it shall be. That's what's the matter with witches; they have nowhere to be. They like places of their own, like ordinary people, and it makes them malignant when they are driven from place to place and given no rights of their own. They are not really interested in human beings, who are so ignorant and clumsy, and resent anyone who is less foolish than themselves: but it annoys them when these stupid creatures interfere with their lives, and they have to get back in their own way.'

'And if we found a witch city,' said Don Guzmán drowsily, for he was really beyond argument and wanted very little save to go to sleep; but he had discovered by now that witches are just as talkative as other women in the moment when a man has no desire save to abandon himself to the sweet refreshment of slumber, 'does that mean you will leave my town alone?'

'How you do harp upon that!' said the witch, with a very ordinary human caress. 'I have never met such a creature for worrying. Haven't I told you?—You have left all that behind you for good and it is no longer any business of yours what goes on down there; all things and all persons that belonged to your stupid life before we met each other are done away with. But in our beautiful city that our children are going to build there'll be singing and dancing in the white streets under the stars and laughter in the taverns; and it'll take more than *rejas* to hold true love out.'

And with that, the thought of Caridad's *rejas*, against which he had leaned on many a weary night, faded for ever from Don Guzmán's mind, and he gasped, on what seemed to be his last breath.

'I'll do it—for my people's sake.'

'Cut the humbug,' murmured the witch, as she sank softly upon him, and loosed across Don Guzmán's eyes the dark flood of her hair. 'You'll do it . . . for mine!'

Now, since the days of Primo de Ribera, there have been many magnificent roads built in Spain: roads along which foreigners in their automobiles may travel from province to province with about a hundredth part of the effort it took Don Guzmán to ride from his own gates to the Silla de las Brujas. And one of these roads, I will not say which, goes looping about a rocky cone upon which, scale upon scale, rise the white houses of a nameless city. The freakish poising of house above house, and the ironic existence of a church spire amid surroundings that seem to have been conceived in a nightmare, alone are enough to suggest witchcraft to the intelligent traveller, who comes upon them for the first time at that hour before sunset when the shadows of the cacti hook themselves about the rocky foundations.

It is the home of a lean and vitiated race, of gaunt men on gaunter horses, and of half-wild, beautiful girls whose eyes it is best not to meet; for thin as has worn the strain of the witches blood in the veins of these descendants of Don Guzmán and his strange mistress, there is something about them which robs the stranger of his certainties, and sends him, if he is prudent, directly on his way.

For the antiquity which breathes from these ancient stones that none save the hands of witches could have fashioned is lethal to the man not reared in its streets, and the whole place carries so evil an air, for all its beauty, that the stranger may puzzle himself to madness, trying to reconcile its diabolism with the mild, indifferent manner of the inhabitants themselves.

So it is better to pass on to that busy and prosperous little township, where, in the market-place, you will find a curious inscription: to the memory of Don Guzmán and the brave souls who, under their Bishop's leadership, gave up their lives to free their city from its plague of witches.

182

□ PIONEERS OF FLIGHT □

Coxwell and Glaisher hang on for dear life during their record flight of 1862.

TALES OF COURAGE

□

PIONEERS OF FLIGHT

□

BY BRIAN WILLIAMS
Illustrated by Francis Phillipps

□

CHERRYTREE BOOKS

A Cherrytree Book

Designed and produced by
A S Publishing

First published 1989
by Cherrytree Press Ltd
a subsidiary of
The Chivers Company Ltd
Windsor Bridge Road
Bath, Avon BA2 3AX

Copyright © Cherrytree Press Ltd 1989

British Library Cataloguing in Publication Data

Williams, Brian
    Pioneers of flight.
    1. Aviation. Biographies. Collections
    I. Title   II. Phillipps, Francis   III. Series
    629.13′092′2

ISBN 0-7451-5054-3

Printed in Italy by New Interlitho

Picture credits: p7, p8, p9 Mary Evans Picture Library; p15, p24, p43 (top) Jean-Loup Charmet; p26 The Illustrated London News Picture Library; p27 bildarchiv preussischer kulturbesitz; p37 OM; p43 Frank Spooner Pictures; p44, p45, p46 Military Archive and Research Services.

□ CONTENTS □

□ PIONEERS OF FLIGHT □

Today, when air travel is commonplace, it is hard to recall that until this century no aeroplane had ever flown. For thousands of years people had dreamed of flying like the birds. A few, perhaps as crazy as they were brave, strapped on birdlike wings and, like Icarus of the Greek legend, attempted to fly. They leaped from towers and clifftops, and fell to their deaths.

According to the legend, Icarus was the son of the inventor Daedalus, who devised wings made from feathers and wax. Together they flew over the Aegean Sea, but Icarus flew too near the sun; its heat melted the wax in his wings and he fell into the sea and was drowned. The example of Icarus was often cited by those who believed that human beings were earthbound by divine intention; to attempt to conquer the air was to court disaster.

Into the unknown

The science of flight did not begin to be understood until 200 years ago. The Chinese flew kites and fired gunpowder rockets, but their ambitions went no further. Leonardo da Vinci drew a sketch of a flapping-wing aeroplane and a helicopter in the 1500s, but no engine had been invented that had the power to lift such aircraft into the air. Not until 1783 when the Montgolfier brothers recognized the lifting properties of hot air, and made a balloon, were human beings at last able to venture into the skies.

It is difficult for a modern person, used to high-speed travel by road and rail, as well as by plane, to understand how brave the first aeronauts must have been. In 1783 the steam railway locomotive and the motor car had not been invented. No one had travelled faster than a horse could gallop. No doctor knew what effect flying might have on the body. The first balloonists soared aloft to explore a strange and unpredictable environment. Many lost their lives.

In 1853 Sir George Cayley, an English scientist, built a curious-looking winged machine. It was based on a model glider he had played with almost 50 years earlier. Sir George wanted to see if this large version would fly with a human passenger. His coachman was told to 'volunteer' for the honour, and the poor man (no doubt quaking in his boots) duly did so. His bravery was no less than that of those who later earned the admiration of the world for their flying exploits.

Defying the doubters

The pioneers of the 1800s were often mocked. Their machines were fanciful and often collapsed spectacularly without ever rising from the ground. Only balloons, and the airships (steerable balloons with engines) that were developed from the 1850s on, seemed able to master the air. It was thanks to the lonely and dangerous researches of men like Otto Lilienthal that knowledge of winged flight advanced, enabling the Wright brothers to make their short, but historic, flight in 1903. Those who followed the Wrights into the air flew in machines that were primitive by today's standards.

In 1910 George Chavez of Peru be-

Balloonists often crash-landed with alarming consequences. This 1906 German aeronaut had a close encounter with a train.

came the first to fly over the European Alps. He flew through the Simplon Pass which is some 2000 metres above sea level (his plane could not climb high enough to fly over the mountains). Tossed violently by swirling air currents, he was in sight of Italy when his machine buckled under the stresses to which it had been subjected. The little Blériot aeroplane simply collapsed, with wings folded, and Chavez tumbled to his death.

In 1919 Ernest Hoy flew over the Canadian Rocky Mountains in a 1914 vintage training aircraft. Its range was laughably short, but somehow Hoy made it, scraping through the Crawford Pass with only a few metres of air between his aircraft and the jagged peaks below. In 1933 the Lady Houston Everest flight took the first aerial photographs of Everest, the world's highest mountain. The two Westland aircraft cleared the peak by just 30 metres.

Flying into danger
Such feats excited public interest in flying. But the general public knew little of the dangers involved. Aero engines were underpowered and unreliable. Bad weather, especially storms and headwinds, could be fatal, since no aircraft could fly high enough to avoid it. Many flyers crashed simply because they were overcome by exhaustion after many hours

Left: Two British Westland aeroplanes took the first air photos of Everest in 1933.

Right: French pilots Charles Nungasser and François Coli disappeared while trying to fly the Atlantic in 1927, in an aircraft like this.

at the controls. On long ocean crossings aircraft sometimes vanished without trace, with no radio or radar to track them. They flew into mountains, crashed on take-off when overweight with extra fuel, became lost in fog or storms.

Without navigational aids, pilots often relied on ground landmarks – following railways or roads, or signs painted on barn roofs. Francis Chichester, flying across the Tasman Sea between Australia and New Zealand in 1931, used a sextant to take sightings of the sun. Experts had said no pilot could handle a sextant and fly at the same time. Even when he reached his stop-over point, the tiny Lord Howe Island, Chichester faced the kind of problem that many air pioneers suffered. His DH Gipsy Moth seaplane sank in a gale and had to be raised and repaired with the assistance of the islanders. Neither they, nor he, knew much – if anything – about how an aeroplane was constructed.

Charles Lindbergh, the first pilot to fly the Atlantic solo, in 1927, was one of many willing to risk such a dangerous journey. On 8 May 1927 two French pilots, Nungasser and Coli, took off from Paris intent on flying from France to the United States. Their biplane had enough fuel for 43 hours, but the wind over the Atlantic was against them, cutting their speed to only 120 km/h. At that slow speed, they would have run out of fuel more than 600 kilometres from the safety of the American coast. Their fate remains unknown.

Their courage, our comfort

There were many examples of amazing courage by men and women aviators during the pioneer years before World War II. In 1931 Ruth Nichols set a new women's altitude record of 8761 metres. Her primitive breathing apparatus consisted of an oxygen tank and a rubber hose. The oxygen was so cold that it froze the inside of her mouth. A month later, she crashed her plane, badly injuring her back. Doctors told her not to fly for a year, but within two months she was back in the air, heavily plastered, for an Atlantic attempt.

Such was the determination that sent aviation pioneers flying round the world, opening up air routes to South America, Asia and Australia. Their pioneer flights made possible the regular international airline services that we take for granted today. After World War II came the jet age, and a new generation of air pioneers: the test pilots. They flew aircraft faster and higher than ever before, into the fringes of space. They experienced the sonic boom and the effects on the human body of high stress forces. They tested ejector seats that were to save the lives of hundreds of jet pilots. Some joined the first corps of astronauts.

As you sit comfortably in your airline seat, watching a film or enjoying the view across the clouds below, remember those who made it possible: the men and women who battled their way into the air. Their courage and perseverance made possible today's age of flying.

THE FIRST AERONAUTS

Could it be true? The watching crowds gasped in amazement as the yellow and blue balloon soared into the sky above Paris. Were men really flying? There was the proof: waving his hat triumphantly, Jean François Pilâtre de Rozier was fulfilling his vow to be the world's first aeronaut.

In 1782 a French papermaker named Joseph Montgolfier flew a model balloon indoors at his home at Avignon. The balloon was made of taffeta over a wooden frame and it was inflated with hot air from some twists of burning paper. From this humble beginning, Joseph and his brother Etienne progressed to bigger balloons that flew outdoors, and on 4 June 1783 they demonstrated their amazing new invention to their neighbours. It was an historic moment. After centuries of failure and disasters, people were about to take to the air. The human dream of imitating birds was, after all, to come true, thanks to the Montgolfiers' genius and the bravery of the first aeronauts.

By July the Montgolfiers were in Paris where they encountered a rival, the hydrogen-gas balloon being tested by Jacques Charles, the brilliant scientist. Charles flew his balloon first, on 27 August, but the Montgolfiers went ahead with their preparations and on 19 September their balloon rose into the skies bearing with it the first aerial passengers – a sheep, a duck and a cock. King Louis XVI and Queen Marie Antoinette were among the marvelling audience.

A young man eagerly sought out the Montgolfiers, pleading to be the first man to ascend in the wonderful balloon. Jean François Pilâtre de Rozier was ready to brave whatever unknown perils the flight might hold for a human. But King Louis had expressly forbidden any person to take part in flying experiments. His advisers warned that flying defied all natural laws: a man might explode in the thin air or go mad.

Pilâtre de Rozier was ready to defy even the royal veto. He was 26, a stout-hearted and scientific young man whose party trick was a fire-eating stunt, using hydrogen gas. A nobleman, the Marquis d'Arlandes, undertook to speak to the king on Pilâtre de Rozier's behalf – provided he too could fly in the Montgolfiers' balloon. Reluctantly, King Louis agreed and the Montgolfiers prepared their new balloon. It was 23 metres high and 15 metres in diameter, with a wickerwork gallery to carry the two aeronauts and an iron fire basket to provide the hot air. Pilâtre de Rozier made several tethered test flights to heights of up to 100 metres in preparation for the great moment – the first free ascent.

The first ascent

The day chosen was 21 November 1783. A huge crowd gathered, many expecting to see the aeronauts suffer a dramatic death. Pilâtre de Rozier and d'Arlandes climbed into the basket beneath the bil-

The ropes were released and the huge crowd gasped as the balloon rose skywards.

lowing balloon. They stood on opposite sides of the gallery, so as to balance the craft. This meant neither man could see the other. When all was ready, Pilâtre de Rozier gave the signal to the Montgolfiers on the ground. It was 1.54 in the afternoon. The tethering ropes were released and at once the balloon rose into the air.

The aeronauts' hearts beat even faster, as the ground receded. Pilâtre de Rozier took a deep breath. The air was sweet, and he shouted with joy. The crowd, at first dumbstruck, burst into wild applause. The flyers doffed their hats and waved as the balloon soared into the sky.

Eager to climb higher, Pilâtre de Rozier urged his companion to throw more straw into the fire basket. Their only precaution against fire was a pail of water and a sponge – to dampen any scorch holes appearing in the balloon fabric. But danger was forgotten in the excitement of the moment. Below them lay Paris, as no one had ever seen it before, the streets and squares jammed with people gazing upward at the astounding sight.

Back to earth – and up again

The flight lasted 25 minutes before the balloon drifted to earth, having travelled almost ten kilometres. As it landed, the balloon collapsed around the aeronauts. A nobleman galloped excitedly to greet them; the three loaded the balloon onto a cart and drove back to Paris and a heroes' welcome.

Pilâtre de Rozier made several more flights, including one with Joseph Mont-

golfier (the inventor's only ascent) and five other passengers.

By 1785 balloonists had a new goal: to cross the English Channel. Pilâtre de Rozier visited London as the guest of the 'British Balloon Club' and met another French flyer, Jean-Pierre Blanchard. He had announced plans for a Channel flight. Pilâtre de Rozier hurried back to France to prepare his own challenge.

Death of an aeronaut

For the Channel crossing, he decided on a combination of a Montgolfier hot air balloon below a hydrogen balloon. Since hydrogen is highly inflammable, the combination of an open fire and the gas was deadly. But Pilâtre de Rozier believed it would give extra height and endurance.

With a companion, Jules Romain, he took off from Boulogne early on a June morning in 1785. The balloon rose to around 1500 metres. Then the horrified spectators (among them Pilâtre de Rozier's English fiancée, Susan Dyer) saw a puff of smoke, followed by a burst of flame. The hydrogen gas caught fire, and the Channel balloon plummeted earthwards. Poor Pilâtre de Rozier was already dead when rescuers ran to the wreck. Romain died within minutes. So too did Susan Dyer, who collapsed from shock. It was a sad end to the life of the world's first intrepid aeronaut.

The spectators could do nothing to save Pilâtre de Rozier and Romain, and the wrecked balloon was rapidly consumed by fire.

□ FLOATING HIGH □

Balloons were to dominate the story of flight for much of the 19th century. Balloon flying became fashionable. But danger was ever-present.

The first balloonists ventured into the sky with courage, but with little knowledge of how to control or navigate their craft. They were blown wherever the wind took them, and even if they did land unscathed they sometimes faced the wrath of an enraged, frightened mob. Several balloons were actually destroyed by villagers fearful of such an 'ungodly machine'.

The Montgolfiers' balloon carried with it the risk of fire, from the burning fire basket. The rival hydrogen balloon was even more dangerous, a flying bomb waiting to explode. But hydrogen was the only lighter-than-air gas available to the early flyers. Modern airships are filled with non-inflammable helium gas.

Only days after Pilâtre de Rozier's historic first flight, Jacques Charles and Nicolas Robert ascended in their hydrogen-filled balloon. Half the population of Paris turned out to watch. Charles wrote afterwards that 'nothing will ever equal that moment of joyous excitement when I felt myself flying away from the earth'. The balloon flew for two hours, before making a perfect landing 43 kilometres from its starting point. Charles was so thrilled he went up again, alone, even though it was after sunset. With only one passenger, the balloon shot up to a height (so Charles guessed) of 3000 metres. He returned safely to earth, but he never flew again.

Across the English Channel

To be blown out across the sea was a balloonist's worst fear, for there was little hope of rescue.

Frenchman Jean-Pierre Blanchard was 31 when, in 1785, he set out to fly the English Channel. His companion (and sponsor) was John Jeffries, a Boston-born doctor. They took off from near Dover on 7 January at 1 pm. Much of their equipment soon had to be jettisoned, as the balloon dropped towards the sea. Over the side went aerial 'oars', anchors and the aeronauts' outer clothing. Blanchard even discarded his trousers, and both men put on cork life-jackets, fearing the worst.

Somehow, however, the balloon remained aloft and at 3 pm it crossed the coast of France. The two aerial pioneers landed in the treetops, some 20 kilometres inland.

Women take to the air

Some of the bravest pioneer balloonists were women. Elizabeth Thible of France was the first woman aloft, flying in a balloon in May 1784. A 14-year-old girl made the first ascent by a woman in England, as a passenger with Blanchard.

Blanchard's wife Sophie was an outstanding flyer. She was said to be happiest floating alone in a balloon, often ascending at night and sleeping in the air. Sophie Blanchard was another victim of the balloonists' greatest enemy: fire. She fell to her death when her balloon caught fire during an aerial firework display in 1817.

Higher and higher

In 1862 the scientist James Glaisher flew with Henry Coxwell, a British balloon pilot, to a height of over 10,000 metres (higher than Mount Everest). In the thin air and with no oxygen apparatus, they found breathing difficult, and could neither move nor speak. Even though he kept losing consciousness, Glaisher went on making scientific observations. Coxwell, his hands frozen, pulled at the release valve with his teeth to begin their descent to the ground. After landing, Glaisher walked 12 kilometres to the nearest town to hire a cart for the balloon!

Such bravery did much to increase scientists' knowledge of the upper air. But balloons would never provide reliable air transport, dependent as they are on the winds. During the 1800s aviation pioneers wrestled with the seemingly insoluble problem of powered flight. Would it only be possible by fitting engines to a balloon – to make an airship? Or, was the answer to imitate the wings of birds and glide?

Blanchard was one of the first professional flyers, making exhibition flights all over Europe and in the USA. This flight over Lille, France, took place shortly after his historic Channel crossing.

□ BIRD-MAN □

Otto Lilienthal envied the birds. As a boy he watched them soaring in the skies and dreamed of imitating their flight. He became the most skilful 'bird-man' of the 1800s.

In 1848, when Otto Lilienthal was born in Germany, no one knew about winged flight. Balloonists drifted with the wind. Steam-driven planes puffed and roared, but failed to get airborne. Lilienthal dreamed of gliding, like the birds. He set out to discover how it could be done, building batlike gliders and testing them himself. Once airborne, he had to discover, and quickly, how to control his glider – or crash. His was a lonely, and very courageous, pioneering path to the skies.

Between 1891 and 1896 Lilienthal built a number of hang-gliders. He made thrilling leaps from hilltops, defying gravity as he swung like a circus trapeze artist below the glider. He built an artificial hill from which to launch himself into the air, his efforts watched by wondering, puzzled onlookers. Most of them thought he was crazy.

Trusting to the air
Lilienthal knew that each flight was risky. He painstakingly checked each strut and wire of the glider before he took off. Strapped into the harness, the taut wings quivering in the breeze, he could feel the glider trying to lift. When he was ready, he launched himself downhill, running to gain take-off speed until with a jerk his feet left the ground. The glider was flying. As the wind sang in the wires,

Lilienthal could gaze down and experience the rare silent thrill of glider flight. His dream had come true: he was flying like the birds.

People were amazed at Lilienthal's daring. But few bystanders could appreciate the dangers, or the extent of his skill. He had learned to 'fly' the hard way, by trial and error, using his body to control the glider. All the time he knew that a sudden gust of wind could be fatal.

Lilienthal might have gone on to build a glider with an engine, the world's first true aeroplane. But the death he had

cheated so long finally caught up with him in August 1896. His monoplane glider flipped over in mid-air and crashed to earth. The great glider pioneer was killed. But others would finish his work.

Others will follow
Lilienthal's courage and persistence inspired a Scottish glider enthusiast, Percy Pilcher. He built his own hang-glider, the *Hawk*. In 1896 Pilcher designed a plane with an engine, but it never flew, for in 1899 he too was killed gliding.

It was left to an American, Octave

Lilienthal seemed to defy gravity as he soared aloft. Each flight was risky, and his body bore bruises from numerous crash landings.

Chanute, to ensure that such courageous deeds were not in vain. Chanute, the author of the first real history of aviation called *Progress in Flying Machines*, also built an improved hang-glider, based on Lilienthal's designs. He became friendly with two young Americans who had notions of their own about how to build flying machines. They were the brothers Wilbur and Orville Wright.

□ THE FIRST FLYERS □

Two young Americans set out to master the science of powered flight. They had begun as bicycle engineers. But their vision and dogged determination took their flying machine into the air one day in December 1903.

Wilbur and Orville Wright ran a bicycle sale and repair business in Dayton, Ohio. One day, Wilbur read a magazine article describing the glider experiments of the German, Otto Lilienthal. He was sure he and his brother could do better. But Lilienthal was dead, killed while gliding.

The history of aviation was littered with tales of brave inventors who had crashed to their deaths in flying machines that simply would not work. Why risk your neck when you could make a living building bicycles?

Nowadays, aircraft are designed and built by huge corporations owning vast factories and laboratories. Thousands of people work on each new design. In the early 1900s the aviation industry did not exist and motor cars were built one by one, by hand. There was nothing to stop Wilbur and Orville from designing their own flying machine – except fear of the

unknown and the ridicule of their neighbours. You had to be crazy to dream of building an aeroplane.

Flying their kites

The Wrights displayed a cool, level-headed courage in tackling the challenge. They dedicated themselves to overcoming the problems, working long hours day and night. They pored over calculations and drawings, and built gliders to see if the theory worked in practice.

The Wrights took their gliders to the Kill Devil sandhills of Kitty Hawk in North Carolina. They travelled there each autumn with the glider in pieces, assembled it and flew it. Then they went home, to work on improvements. Their third glider, flown in 1902, had done well. But could such a machine be fitted with an engine and still fly?

The Wrights are proved right

Other inventors, such as fellow American Samuel Pierpoint Langley, were known to be working on aircraft designs. The newspapers reported crashes and accidents involving 'flying machines'. Few people really believed these weird machines would actually ever work.

Wilbur and Orville kept working steadily. They built their own petrol engine (no existing engine was light enough). They designed and made the

The Wrights' gliders looked like huge box-kites. The brothers gained valuable experience from flying these flimsy-looking aircraft.

twin airscrews for their new machine. They even constructed a wind tunnel to test the wing shape. By late 1903 they were ready to try it out in the air.

The brothers took their machine, named *Flyer*, to the Kill Devil hills. It was a lonely spot, away from prying eyes. There were no cheering crowds, no journalists. On 14 December Wilbur stretched out in the pilot's position on the flimsy wing. The engine fired, but the *Flyer* would not lift off the ground. It was a setback, but the Wrights did not give up easily. On 17 December they tried again.

This time Orville was to be the pilot. Both men were dressed smartly, in suits, starched collars and caps. Together, they checked the *Flyer* for the last time, fiddled with the engine. Then they talked quietly for a moment and shook hands. It might be their last handshake . . .

It was a cold, windy day with rain in the air. At 10.30 in the morning, Wilbur raised a flag to give the signal. Flat on his stomach on the left (port) wing, Orville waved to show he was ready and released the wire holding the aircraft on to its launch rail. Wilbur ran alongside to hold the right wing steady, fearing a sudden gust of wind that would send the craft careering sideways. Orville stared ahead through the humming wires, his heart beating faster. The *Flyer* seemed suddenly to have a life of its own.

The machine ran along the launch rail for about 15 metres at a little over a fast walking pace. And then it lifted into the air. Orville felt the motion change, as the machine left the ground and took to the

Orville and Wilbur took turns to pilot the Flyer *on the first exhilarating flights. The longest that day in 1903 lasted just 59 seconds.*

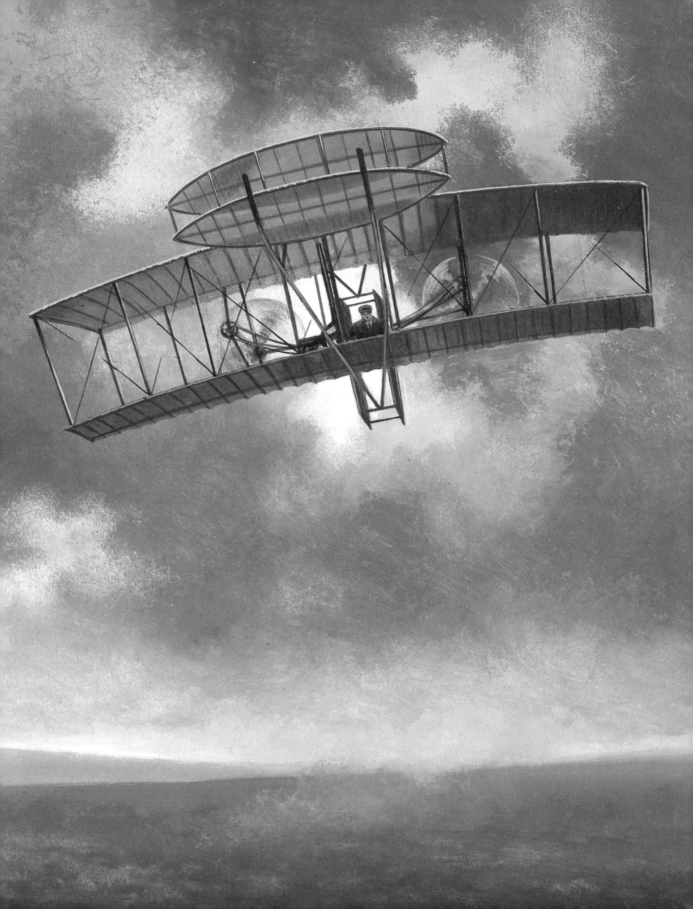

air under its own power. Wilbur released the wing and the *Flyer* flew. It rose to a height of only three metres, dipped, then climbed again before diving to the ground some 37 metres away.

Wilbur dashed to greet his brother, who climbed from the aircraft, breathless but grinning. Only five other people (from the nearby lifeboat station) watched the Wrights make history.

Triumphant, the brothers were eager to try again. The *Flyer* flew three more times that day. On the last flight, Wilbur flew for 260 metres. Then the brothers packed up, sent a telegram home, and returned to work. The world had entered a new age.

Showing the world

Flying in a balloon or airship (which floats) was very different from flying in an aeroplane, which is heavier than air and needs to be trimmed (balanced) exactly if it is not to crash headlong. Lift, thrust, drag: these were all unknown forces, to be investigated and understood. No one knew how to fly an aeroplane safely. How

On 17 September 1908 Orville was badly injured when his plane crashed. His passenger, US Army Lieutenant William Selfridge, was killed.

did you climb? Turn? Slow down? How high could you fly? How fast? Every landing was a new adventure, every take-off a renewed challenge to the pilot's courage and skill.

The Wrights were soon venturing higher and staying aloft longer. In 1908 Wilbur took their new biplane to Europe and astonished everyone with his daring, flying for as long as two and a half hours, and even carrying passengers.

Other aviators followed where the Wrights had led the way. Soon aeroplanes were taking to the air across the United States and Europe, their pilots inspired by the pioneers of Kitty Hawk. After 1912 Orville Wright worked alone, for Wilbur fell ill with typhoid fever and died. Orville sold the business in 1915, and left aviation to others. He died in 1948, having seen the dawning of a new age: that of jets and rockets.

□ DARING TO BE FIRST □

The Wrights had proved that the aeroplane could fly. In the years following their success, a small band of brave men and women followed them into the skies. These pioneer pilots had the courage to go where few others dared.

The race across the Channel

To fly over the sea in a machine made of wood and fabric, driven by a small, unreliable petrol engine, called for real determination. Yet only six years after the Wrights' first flight, aviators were pitting themselves against this challenge.

The English Channel is not a wide waterway (you can see the white cliffs of Dover from France on a clear day), but its bad weather is notorious. It was a formidable barrier for the early aeroplanes and a psychological challenge for their pilots. Many people still believed the aeroplane was a toy, a kind of outsize kite with a propeller. The British *Daily Mail* newspaper offered a cash prize for the first pilot brave (or foolhardy) enough to fly the Channel.

Among the leading pilots in Europe was Hubert Latham (French but of English descent). He took off from France on 19 July 1909 in an Antoinette aircraft with a tiny 50-hp engine. Eighteen kilometres out from Sangatte, the engine cut out and Latham glided down to crash-land in the sea. Fortunately, the weather was calm and he sat on his floating aircraft, smoking a cigarette, until a rescue boat reached him.

Down, but not drowned: Hubert Latham awaits rescue in the English Channel.

□ Louis Blériot □

Blériot landed in a field near Dover Castle. Flag-waving early risers greeted his spectacular arrival.

Next to try was Louis Blériot (bankrupt and nursing a foot burned by a hot exhaust pipe during an earlier flight). His monoplane had an engine even smaller than Latham's and his only guide to a safe landing place in England was a picture postcard sent by a friendly reporter.

Blériot took off at 4.41 in the morning of 25 July, crutches strapped to the side of the plane! 'Now I thought only of my machine . . .', he recalled later. Were his tiny engine to fail, he knew he could not glide down, since the plane could fly no higher than a few metres above the water. He must have listened anxiously to the engine's beat as he sat in the open cockpit, head and shoulders exposed above the flimsy, fabric-covered fuselage, peering over the wing and past the whirling propeller for sight of land.

He followed three ships heading for Dover, to make sure he did not lose his way and fly out into the bleak North Sea. Ahead lay the formidable 100-metre-high Shakespeare Cliff at Dover; Blériot's plane could not fly above such an obstacle, so he had to sideslip through a gap in the cliff edge before touching down in a field. It was 5.18. He had flown from France to England (38 kilometres) in just 37 minutes.

First across the USA

The years before World War I were the years when pilots attempted the impossible almost every time they took off. No pilot surmounted more mishaps, in the air and on the ground, than Calbraith Perry Rodgers – the first man to fly across the United States.

The year was 1911. Rodgers' plane was a Wright machine, named the *Vin Viz Flyer*. His plan was to fly from New York to California, in a series of 'hops'. He would have to find fields to land in (there were hardly any airstrips) and pick his way across a continent. He aimed to follow the railroad, to show that aeroplanes were the future as far as transcontinental travel was concerned.

Rodgers' resolution was sorely tested. On only the second leg of his flight, he crashed into a chicken coop, and his plane had to be rebuilt by the Wrights' mechanic, Charlie Taylor.

Rodgers battled on against a series of setbacks. A spark plug popped loose from the engine, and he had to fly one-handed while holding it in place. He became lost in a thunderstorm, flying through crackling lightning. He suffered some 70 crashes before, after 84 days, he reached his destination, limping from the battered aircraft on crutches. His aeroplane had been practically rebuilt en route; only the rudder was left intact. But Rodgers had made it.

Women Aloft

The first woman pilot was Raymonde de Laroche of France. She was taught to fly in 1909 by Charles Voisin, the great French aircraft designer, when she was just 23 years old. In those days there was no dual control system for teaching pilots. The student sat in the cockpit at the controls while the instructor called out instructions from the ground. Once in the air, and out of earshot, the learner was alone with the aircraft and the elements. Flying needed a lot of nerve. It was dangerous, Raymonde de Laroche agreed, but she regarded it as simply packing all the hazards of a lifetime into a few hours or minutes.

Other women pilots followed her lead. In 1911 American journalist Harriet Quimby became the first licensed woman pilot in the United States. Her friend Mathilde Moisant became number two, even though her brother John had met his death in a flying accident.

The daring Harriet Quimby
Harriet Quimby believed in flying, both as a sport and as the transport of the future. In 1912 she travelled to England to attempt a cross-Channel flight, determined to show everyone what women pilots could achieve.

Harriet Quimby in her flying clothes. She believed flying offered women new opportunities.

She had been flying for a year only. She had no experience of flying over the open sea, or of navigation. It must have been daunting, waiting to take off on a damp, cold April day. She shivered, in spite of the extra clothing she was wearing beneath her flying suit. Friends gave her a hot water bag to strap around her middle to ward off the cold. She was also shown how to use a compass. Then she was in the air – and on her own.

Bad weather for flying

Unlike Blériot, Harriet Quimby was unlucky with the Channel weather. She flew into a cold, dense fog. She could see neither sky ahead nor sea below: she had little chance of following the tugboat that was supposed to act as her guide. Getting lost would be disastrous. Her plane had little fuel reserves and if she was forced down into the sea she would be lucky to survive long in the freezing water. She climbed higher to find a break in the fog – but fuel flooded the carburettor and her engine misfired. Her heart sank; below her was the cold grey Channel.

As the tiny plane spiralled downwards, she peered through her goggles at the waves, white-capped and menacing. But then the engine revived and she came out of fog into sunlight. The Blériot skimmed low over the waves and to Harriet's intense relief she spotted the French coast. She managed to land on the beach, some 40 kilometres off-course from her target, Calais, and was greeted by a cheering crowd of fishermen.

Sadly, in July of that same year Harriet Quimby was killed while giving an exhibition flight near Boston. Her plane went into a sudden dive and both she and her passenger were flung out and killed.

THE AIRSHIP AVIATORS

A German engineer, Count Ferdinand von Zeppelin, pioneered the airship. The German Zeppelin crews of World War I faced hardship and danger high in the sky.

The most advanced Zeppelins flew very high to avoid enemy fighter planes – up to 7000 metres. They were huge (more than 200 metres long) but slow, cruising through the clouds at less than 150 km/h, rather like vast aerial whales. The crews of these monsters endured constant biting wind and freezing cold. Inside the gondolas, suspended beneath the vast gas envelope, the men wore layers of thick clothing, with newspapers stuffed inside for extra warmth.

Because of the risk of explosion from the highly inflammable hydrogen gas in the airship's gas cells, cooking was forbidden. The men ate cold sausage and bread, supplemented by chemically self-heating cans of stew. At maximum height, the men suffered from altitude sickness, becoming so weak they could move only with difficulty. Occasionally an airship commander might order a below-cloud observation, lowering a man in a small gondola at the end of a long cable – surely one of the most perilous and uncomfortable of duties!

The airship was developed in the 1800s by pioneers such as Henri Giffard and Alberto Santos-Dumont. It had the advantages of long range and endurance, but a basic weakness in the dangerous hydrogen used to inflate it. Several tragic accidents brought the age of airship travel to an end in the 1930s.

Zeppelin crews suffered from altitude sickness and numbing cold. They faced the threat of enemy bombs from above and machine-gun fire from below.

27

▫ AEROPLANES CAN MAKE IT ▫

Few people believed the flimsy aeroplanes of the 1910-1920 era could fly an ocean or cross the polar wastes. Only the pilots, willing it to be possible, believed aeroplanes could make it. They opened the way for our comfortable airline services.

Flying the Atlantic today, a passenger sits high above the clouds and weather in a pressurized metal cabin. In six or seven hours, or less by Concorde, the Atlantic is crossed. No one in the jet may even have glimpsed the ocean. It was very different for the crews of three American flying boats who set off in May 1919 from Long Island.

A flying boat had one big advantage over a landplane; it could touch down on the water if it ran out of fuel – if the sea was calm enough. The US Navy's NC-

The US Navy flying boats ride out the Atlantic storms.

Alcock and Brown take off from Newfoundland for their 16½-hour flight to Ireland.

class flying boats did not have the range to fly the Atlantic non-stop. They had to fly in legs, stopping to refuel. Fifty-seven naval ships were positioned across the ocean to aid the flyers if they came down.

The Atlantic proved a violent opponent. Two of the flying boats were forced out of the flight by bad weather and mechanical problems. One was abandoned at sea; the other had to taxi, using engine power, through rolling seas for 48 hours before reaching the Azores. Only one aircraft, NC-4, commanded by Lt-Commander Albert Read, completed the crossing, touching down first in Portugal and then in England, on 31 May.

□ ALCOCK AND BROWN □

Two weeks later, on 14 June 1919, two British flyers, John Alcock and Arthur Whitten Brown, set off from Newfoundland. Their aim was to fly the Atlantic non-stop. There were to be no watery touchdowns for them, for their aircraft was a landplane, a Vickers Vimy bomber, with twin engines. The Vimy had a maximum range of 3900 kilometres. Would this be enough? Ahead lay 3000 kilometres of ocean, and then Ireland,

their planned landing point.

The airmen's black cat mascot dolls, Twinkletoes and Lucky Jim, did not at first bring them much luck. They flew into fog, with thick cloud above. Their radio broke, and after an exhaust snapped on one engine the noise was so great neither man could hear the other shout.

The Vimy battles through

They flew very low (compared to modern planes) at between 1000 and 2000 metres and of course far slower – around 190 km/h. Pilots had no instruments for 'blind' flying, so any large cloud posed real problems. For a time they had no idea where they were, until they climbed above the cloud into clear skies and were able to take a navigational sun sighting. It was bitterly cold. Brown had to stand up in the open cockpit to scrape snow off the fuel-flow indicators. Even the coffee in their flasks was little comfort.

At half past eight in the morning of 15 June, they sighted Ireland and because the weather was bad decided to land the moment they could. What looked like a green field turned out to be a soft bog, and the Vimy ended up with its tail in the air – an undignified end to an epic flight.

□ ATLANTIC ALONE □

Charles Lindbergh was the first person to make the long, dangerous Atlantic crossing alone. The danger of crashing at take-off, the risk of engine failure over the ocean, the likelihood that a lone pilot would fall victim to sheer weariness; all these were perils to be challenged and overcome.

It was 20 May 1927. Shortly after dawn, Charles Lindbergh had taken off from Roosevelt Field, New York. His destination: Europe. Before him lay the Atlantic Ocean and a flight into history.

As the small monoplane droned on through the empty skies above the Atlantic, Lindbergh had plenty of time to ponder over his chances of ever reaching land. Ahead lay vast stretches of cold, empty ocean. He had planned the flight with care, but so many things could go wrong. And there was no one to help if trouble struck.

A flying fuel tank

At least his plane, the *Spirit of St Louis*, was his own choice for the flight. He had wanted a single-engined plane because it offered longer range. But if that one engine should fail, thousands of kilometres from land . . .

Lindbergh was confident it would not. Today, when aircraft are bigger, faster and crammed with electronic navigation aids unknown in the 1920s, twin-engined jets must follow strict routes over long sea flights. Most transatlantic airliners have three or four engines. Lindbergh had no such safety margin.

Sitting on his wicker seat in the cramped cockpit (dimensions just 94 cm wide by 81 cm long by 130 cm high), Lindbergh could not even see where he was going. His only forward vision was through a periscope. The *Spirit of St Louis* was a flying fuel tank, with extra tanks fitted to give it the range to fly the Atlantic. The extra fuel was stored in front of the pilot, blocking his forward view. Lindbergh had asked for this: he felt safer with the fuel in front, fearful that a tank behind him might be forced forwards and crush him in the event of a crash landing.

He knew that if it were to succeed, his flight would be a marathon of endurance. His only supplies consisted of two bottles of water and some sandwiches to sustain him over a distance of 5800 kilometres – roughly twice the distance flown by Alcock and Brown in 1919.

The aircraft carried enough fuel for 40 hours' flying when it took off at 7.50 in the morning of 20 May. Take-off was probably the most dangerous moment of such long-distance flights; weighed down by extra fuel, the aircraft rose uncertainly into the air, gaining height painfully slowly. Other flyers had met disaster at this point, so Lindbergh was relieved when the *Spirit of St Louis* was safely aloft and cruising eastwards.

Lindy's lonely odyssey

Lindbergh was attempting the dream of pioneer aviators. An Atlantic solo crossing would prove not only the reliability of the aeroplane, but also the dependability

Lindbergh sat hunched inside this tiny cockpit for 27 hours. He could see out of the aircraft only through a periscope or a side window.

of the human in the cockpit. But a lone pilot faced the ever-growing danger of exhaustion. Lindbergh, an experienced flyer with the US Mail, knew the dangers of falling asleep at the controls. There was no automatic pilot to take over in those days.

As he left Newfoundland behind and headed out over the Atlantic, his mind began to wander. Would he forget to switch between fuel tanks (to keep the plane balanced)? The engine seemed to be running rough, but he found it hard to concentrate on the rhythm. He was getting so sleepy . . .

He slapped his face, forcing his eyelids upwards with his fingertips, leaned out of the cabin window so that the blast of freezing air shocked him back to wakefulness.

Having regained control of his weary senses, Lindbergh made himself work. He checked the wind, rechecked his course, scanned the clouds through his periscope. The flight seemed endless; it was as if he had flown into a dream-world, remote from reality. What am I doing here? he mused. Can I endure this? How much longer?

From the time he left New York,

Lindbergh had no means of contacting the world. His plane had no radio. There was no means of tracking it (radar was not yet invented). Unless a ship spotted him, he would be lost to view until he landed – if he landed. Bad weather was the worst enemy. If he was forced off course, he could become disorientated, lost in cloud, circling vainly until his fuel ran out and the engine died.

Lindbergh's flight was a triumph of willpower. He flew through rain, storm winds, fog, even snow. At times the *Spirit of St Louis* flew only 30 metres above the water – Lindbergh became anxious that he might hit an iceberg and climbed to 3000 metres until bad weather forced him down again. He could see porpoises in the sea beneath him. At one point he began seeing 'mirages' of coastlines that were not there.

He could think only of sleep, and of stretching his aching limbs. He had been alone in the cockpit for 27 hours without seeing a sign of human life. At home people had gone to bed, got up, gone about their day's work, while he flew on, always on.

Land ahoy!

The sight of fishing boats cheered him immensely. Europe must be close. He circled the boats, calling from the open cockpit: 'Which way to Ireland?'. There

was no answer, no crewman even appeared on deck. It was eerie.

At last, after 16 hours flying across unbroken ocean, he spotted land, real land. It was Ireland. Another fishing boat, and a friendly wave from a startled fisherman as the plane roared overhead. He had made it!

Turning southeast, he crossed the English Channel and flew over the coast of France. It was now the evening of 21 May. Darkness was falling but Lindbergh's aircraft had been spotted, and people were streaming out of Paris to greet him. At 10.22 pm the *Spirit of St Louis* dropped down from the night sky and landed on the airfield of Le Bourget.

The epic flight had taken 33½ hours.

The plane rolled to a halt, the engine died. The lights of cars and flashbulbs flared in the darkness. Charles Lindbergh, the flyer who had braved the wide ocean alone, climbed out of the cockpit and into the limelight. He was now the most famous man in the world.

One sad consequence of Lindbergh's fame was the kidnapping of his baby son in 1932. The stolen child was found dead.

Lindbergh was cheered by excited crowds as he walked stiffly from the plane and into the glare of publicity that was to last for the rest of his life.

□ WINGS ACROSS THE OCEAN □

By the 1930s some of the basic problems of flight had been tackled. The pioneers of aviation had advanced a little, but there was still an immense way to go.

Courageous pilots, some with surprisingly little experience, set out to cross oceans and deserts, flying over mountains and forests, even over the Arctic and the high Himalayas. The dangers they faced were many: fatigue, engine failure, running out of fuel, simply getting lost without radio or radar to guide them and with very few airstrips to head for in an emergency.

□ THE AEROPLANE GIRL □

Amy Johnson was Britain's 'air queen' of the 1930s. She learned to fly in 1929, and only a year later embarked on a flight that would have deterred a pilot with years of experience. She planned to fly from Britain to Australia! Amy Johnson believed in aviation. She was willing to give up her job, and risk her life, to show the world that a lone pilot could open up an air route that thousands of passengers would one day be able to fly in comfort.

Her plane was a tiny green-painted Gipsy Moth, named *Jason*. Her planned route was to take her across two continents and some of the wildest country on earth. There would be few airstrips to land on, and little chance of rescue should she come down in desolate mountains or tropical jungle. On the map it looked forbidding enough; from England

*Destination Australia: Amy Johnson
prepares for departure from Croydon
Aerodrome, England.*

35

across Europe and the Middle East, across India to Bangkok and Singapore, and finally south over the islands of the East Indies and the open sea to Australia. She left England on 5 May 1930, cheered by a small crowd of friends and well-wishers.

Today, it is hard to imagine the problems Amy Johnson faced. She had to hand-pump almost 200 litres of fuel each day. She was a skilled mechanic (mostly self taught) but was forced to argue with male engineers before they would let her near the engine during refuelling stops! Her plane could fly no higher than 3000 metres, yet many of the mountains on her route were above this height. She had to find a path between the peaks.

Sand, sun and sharks

Each leg of her journey brought new dangers. While flying across the Syrian desert her plane flew into a sandstorm. Whirling clouds of sand billowed upwards, blinding her, forcing her to make an emergency landing before sand grains choked the engine. In Burma a damaged wing had to be patched with shirt material borrowed from a local tailor. By the time she reached Singapore, her face was burnt brick-red by the sun and she was exhausted. Worst of all, the most difficult stage of the flight – over Indonesia and the Java Sea – still lay ahead. At one landing strip in the dense jungle, fuel cans were carried to the plane by donkey and she had to filter the petrol herself to make sure it was safe to use. On the last leg, she had to cross the open ocean to reach northern Australia; she flew 800 nerve-racking kilometres over seas notorious for sharks. Finally she landed at Darwin on 24 May 1930.

Amy Johnson made other daring long-distance flights, including some with her husband Jim Mollison. She remained a celebrity of the air until her death in a wartime flying accident in 1941.

□ BERYL MARKHAM □

Imagine diving seaward, with no engine, trying desperately to turn on the reserve fuel tank of your plane! This was the situation British flyer Beryl Markham faced in 1936. And she was alone above the Atlantic.

In the 1930s a small aircraft flying the Atlantic could easily be blown off course by strong head winds. Blowing directly against the aircraft's course, these winds could also slow down the airspeed so much that the aircraft ran out of fuel long before land was in sight. When Beryl Markham took off from Abingdon, England, in 1936 her Vega Gull aircraft had enough fuel for 24 hours at a speed of 240 km/h – provided there was no headwind. She was trying to be the first woman to fly the Atlantic solo from east to west. Only Jim Mollinson had done so, and he had started further west, from Ireland.

Soon after take-off, Beryl Markham found herself flying into a 65 km/h headwind. She battled on, grimly holding her course into the wind, yet aware that she was using more fuel than planned. Four hours after taking off, the engine stopped. In darkness, she groped for a torch to help her find the tap of the reserve fuel tank. The plane was only 70 metres above the waves when she found the tap, and the engine roared back to life.

1930s aerial elegance: Beryl Markham symbolized the glamour of flying.

She had been in the air for more than 19 hours before she at last sighted the coast of Newfoundland. It was none too soon, for the engine was spluttering ominously. With a virtually empty fuel tank, the plane limped over the shoreline and crash-landed nose-first in a swamp. Beryl Markham managed to climb out of the cockpit. She was exhausted and waist-deep in mud when rescued by fishermen.

□ GATTY AND POST □

In June 1931 American pilot Wiley Post, with Australian navigator Harold Gatty, flew around the world – a distance of more than 27,000 kilometres – in 8 days 15 hours 51 minutes.

In their single-engined Lockheed Vega monoplane, Post and Gatty took off from Roosevelt Field, New York. They headed east with stops in Britain and Germany before the long flight across Russia. Ahead lay the wastes of Siberia and the frozen ocean around Alaska. In Canada they were forced to take off from a road because an airfield was flooded.

By their remarkable feat of endurance (and engine reliability) Post and Gatty proved that aeroplanes had the potential to fly regular passenger routes.

□ ON A WING AND A PRAYER □

One of the most famous record-breaking pilots was Charles Kingsford Smith of Australia. In May 1935 he and navigator Gordon Taylor took off in the *Southern Cross* for an airmail flight to New Zealand, crossing the Tasman Sea.

It should have been a routine trip, but after 900 kilometres one of the aircraft's two engines failed, forcing them to turn back. Then the overworked port engine began to overheat, burning oil and losing power. The two men dumped cargo and excess fuel to save weight, but the plane gradually lost height until it was almost touching the waves.

Somehow they had to get oil into the engine. While Kingsford Smith flew as steadily as he could, Taylor crawled out of the cockpit with a vacuum flask of oil. He inched his way out along the wing, holding on grimly to the flask.

He did the same thing five times, every 35 minutes, topping up the sick engine with oil before the *Southern Cross* landed safely after 16 hours in the air.

□ AMERICA'S FLYING HEROINE □

It was 1932. Alone in a small aircraft, the grey ocean surging beneath her, Amelia Earhart braved the angry elements. Many pilots believed that no woman could fly solo over long distances. Earhart was determined to prove the doubters wrong.

Climb! Climb! As the storm buffeted her plane above the cold Atlantic Ocean, Amelia Earhart remembered the words of her flying instructor. Climb! Get above the bad weather – if you can. Since gaining her pilot's licence in 1922 (when there were fewer than 20 women pilots in the world) Amelia Earhart had tackled a number of aerial challenges. She was one of a small but determined and skilful band of women aviators, whose record-breaking feats were even more remarkable because of the incredible physical demands long-distance flights made on a solo pilot.

Amelia Earhart is remembered above all for one flight, the solo crossing of the North Atlantic she made in 1932. As she piloted her Lockheed Vega eastwards she must often have thought of those who had said 'it can't be done, not by a woman!'

First woman to fly the Atlantic
Amelia Earhart was a born daredevil. Her mother had been the first woman to climb Pike's Peak, a mountain in Colorado, USA, and Amelia inherited her adventurous spirit. From a young girl she had been entranced by the adventure of flight.

She had learned to fly and in 1928 she had become the first woman to cross the Atlantic in an aeroplane, as a passenger on board a Fokker Trimotor. After 20 hours in the air, the seaplane landed off the coast of Wales, and the aviators were surprised to find that for some time no one took any notice of them!

Determined to show that women could be pilots as well as passengers on long-distance flights, Amelia Earhart decided to fly the Atlantic herself – alone. Her husband, publisher George Putnam, helped buy her 'dream plane', a red-painted Lockheed Vega with a range of just over 5000 kilometres. It was the right aircraft for the flight, but even so the prospect was daunting. If Atlantic seas were wild, Atlantic weather was often wilder, and only two flyers (both men, Charles Lindbergh and Bert Hinkler) had so far flown the Atlantic alone. For a lone pilot the risks of accident or falling asleep at the controls were real on such a long flight, so far from land.

Braving the storm's force
'Do you think I can make it?' Earhart asked her friend and technical adviser Bernt Balchen as she squeezed herself into the pilot's seat. He nodded. But everyone knew what risks she was taking. Amelia remained calm, grabbing a last nap as the mechanics made the final adjustments to the Vega's engine and checked the extra fuel tanks in the wings and cabin.

Alone above the cold, stormy Atlantic Ocean, Earhart knew she stood little chance if the Vega's engine were to fail.

Amelia Earhart travelled light. Her few in-flight comforts included an elephant's foot bracelet for luck, a silk scarf, a screwdriver for punching holes in tomato juice cans, a flask of soup, smelling salts (to keep awake), and a powder compact so she could 'look nice when the reporters come'.

On 20 May 1932 the Lockheed took off from Harbour Grace, Newfoundland. Amelia Earhart flew light: soup and cans of tomato juice were her only food supply: 'Extra food would have been extra weight'. She also took smelling salts, hoping that sniffing them would stop her from falling asleep. If she were to crash into the sea, her main hope was to signal to a passing ship with an emergency flare.

Cruising at 4000 metres, Amelia could enjoy the sunset. The engine droned reassuringly as she set course eastwards, knowing it would be many hours before she could relax her concentration.

Before long, problems began. As well as fighting off tiredness, she had to cope with the discomforts of the cramped cabin and with the sickening smell of hot oil from the engine. Only hours after take-off, the plane's altimeter had failed, so for most of the flight she had no idea how high she was flying. Flames burst from a broken welding in the engine exhaust. The fire alarmed her, but even worse was the nerve-shattering vibration throughout the cabin. To add to her difficulties, there was yet another danger; the Atlantic weather.

Wild weather

The aircraft of the 1930s flew through the weather, not above it like today's jets. They were tossed and spun like leaves in the wind. As Earhart's Vega battled onwards, it pitched wildly and she had difficulty keeping control. Rain lashed the windscreen, so that she could barely see the aircraft's propeller. Struggling to stay on course, she climbed higher to seek clearer weather. But to her horror she saw ice beginning to form on the wings. Icing could be fatal. If ice overloaded the wings, the plane would become unstable and crash. She must lose height again. Diving seawards in a near-vertical spin, back into the storm, the Vega narrowly escaped disaster, levelling out only metres above the waves. Thankfully, she gained height again.

The storm finally relented and the Vega's engine never faltered (despite the broken weld, the flames and the smell). Weariness was now the main threat. Amelia resorted to the smelling salts whenever she felt sleep threatening. Her body ached, the pilot's seat now felt hard and unyielding.

At last she glimpsed a smudge of green on the horizon below – land. After 13½ hours, the Lockheed came down safely in a farmer's field at Culmore in Ireland. Amelia Earhart had flown the Atlantic, and she had done so faster than either Lindbergh or Hinkler. Having only the clothes she flew in, Amelia treated herself to a shopping spree when she reached London, where the celebrations began.

Triumphs and Disaster

After her epic flight, Earhart was the most celebrated woman pilot in the world. She was eager to accept new challenges. In 1935 she made the first solo flight from Hawaii to California in 18 hours. In 1937 she set off with co-pilot Fred Noonan to fly around the world in a specially equipped Lockheed Electra.

On such long flights, safety margins were narrow. Exact navigation was essential if landfalls were to be found amid the vast Pacific Ocean. Bad weather, poor visibility, instrument failure, fuel miscalculation: any of these could be fatal. On a 4000-kilometre leg across the Pacific, radio contact with the aircraft was lost after 15¼ hours. The Lockheed had vanished. No trace of it, or of Amelia Earhart and Fred Noonan, was ever found. The most likely answer to the mystery is that she became lost in fog, missing the island where she was due to land, and crashed into the sea when the plane's fuel ran out.

The Lockheed Electra made 28 stops on Earhart's round-the-world trip, some, like this one, enforced. Engineers worked round the clock to do repairs.

☐ HIGH FLYERS ☐

Ader, Clément French pioneer of flight. His *Eole* aeroplane is reported to have 'hopped' 50 metres in 1890.

Alcock, John and **Brown, Arthur Whitten** British pilots who made the first non-stop flight across the Atlantic (1919).

Barnstormers Daredevil stunt flyers of the 1920s who thrilled crowds by low-level flying, aerobatics and displays including wing-walking and stunts in which people transferred from one plane to another in mid-air.

Batten, Jean New Zealander who was the first woman to fly across the dangerous Tasman Sea and in 1936 flew from England to New Zealand in 11 days.

Blanchard, Jean-Pierre French balloonist, first to fly the English Channel (1785). Made the first balloon ascent in the USA from Philadelphia on 9 January 1793 – his 45th flight.

Blanchard, Sophie French balloonist, wife of Jean-Pierre Blanchard. Made her first ascent in 1805. Killed in 1817 when her balloon caught fire.

Blériot, Louis French pilot who made the first flight across the English Channel in an aeroplane (1909).

Byrd, Richard US explorer, first to fly over the North Pole, with Floyd Bennett, in 1926. Also first to fly over the South Pole (with three companions) in 1929.

Cayley, Sir George British glider pioneer of the early 1800s, who flew models and tested a man-carrying version in 1853.

Cobham, Sir Alan British aviator who in the 1920s flew around Africa, from Cape Town to London, from London to Rangoon, and from England to Australia and back. Also pioneered in-flight refuelling.

Cochran, Jacqueline US flyer, first woman to break the sound barrier (1953); set 1974 women's speed record of 2300 km/h.

Cody, Samuel US pilot who made first aeroplane flight in Great Britain, 16 October 1908.

Coleman, Bessie First black woman pilot, who went from the USA to France in order to learn. Killed flying in an air show in 1926.

Costes, Didier French flyer, first to fly non-stop across South Atlantic, from Senegal to Brazil (3220 km in 19 hr 50 min, 1927).

Coxwell, Henry British balloonist, made a high-altitude-ascent in 1862, flying higher than Mt Everest.

Curtiss, Glenn First US pilot to fly more than a kilometre in public (1908); invented the seaplane (1911).

Davies, E. Trehawke First woman to fly the English Channel, as a passenger with Gustav Hamel (1912).

Defries, Colin First man to fly an aeroplane in Australia (1909).

Dirigible Steerable airship; the first fully controllable dirigible was the *La France* of Renard and Krebs (1884).

Doolittle, James H. US pilot who made the first

Amelia Earhart – most famous of all women pilots.

coast-to-coast flight across the USA in a single day (1922). The first non-stop crossing of the USA was by O.G. Kelly and J.A. Macready in 1923 (4050 km in 26 hr 50 min).

Earhart, Amelia Most famous of all women flyers; first woman to fly the Atlantic solo.

Farman, Henry British/French designer of some of the best early aeroplanes.

Garnerin, André Jacques French inventor of the first practical parachute (1797). His niece Eliza became the world's first female professional parachute jumper.

Glaisher, James Scientist who made a record balloon ascent with Coxwell at the age of 53, and died the same year as the Wrights flew (1903).

Hargrave, Lawrence Australian inventor of the box-kite (1893).

Henson, W. S. British inventor of the Aerial Steam Carriage, an unsuccessful aeroplane of 1842-43.

Hinkler, Bert Australian pilot. First to fly solo from England to Australia (1928), second pilot to cross the Atlantic solo. Killed 1933.

Hunefeld, Baron von German leader of first flight east to west across the Atlantic (1928);

36½ hours in the air from Ireland to the Straits of Belle Isle (Newfoundland/Labrador).

Johnson, Amy British pilot whose epic flights of the 1930s made her an international celebrity. Flew solo from Britain to Australia. Set a 1936 record for the flight of 3 days 16½ hours.

Kingsford Smith, Sir Charles Australian aviation pioneer, first to fly from USA to Australia (11,700 km) in 1928.

Langley, Samuel Pierpoint US designer of the *Aerodrome*, which fell into the Potomac River in 1903 as it was launched.

Laroche, Raymonde de French baroness, first woman to hold a pilot's licence (1910).

Law, Ruth US flyer, first woman to loop the loop and a record-breaker of the 1916 era.

Lindbergh, Charles US pilot, first to fly the Atlantic solo (1927).

Markham, Beryl Kenya-based flyer who flew the North Atlantic solo in September 1936, crossing in 21½ hours from Abingdon, England to Nova Scotia.

Maxim, Sir Hiram British designer of a flying

Charles Kingsford Smith vanished in 1935 flying his Lady Southern Cross *from India to Singapore.*

Ruth Nichols, one of America's foremost 'petticoat pilots'. Her fur coat was no luxury in a freezing cockpit.

machine which just failed to fly in 1894.

Mock, Jerrie American flyer, the first woman to fly solo around the world (1964).

Mollison, Jim British aviator of the 1930s, flew the Atlantic from east to west. Married to Amy Johnson for a time.

Money, Major John English balloonist who was blown out across the North Sea in 1785 and spent five hours clinging to the wreckage before being picked up by a revenue cutter.

Nichols, Ruth American flyer who became known as the 'Flying Deb' and set many flying records between 1928 and 1931. The first woman to land in every one of the then 48 states of the USA.

Norton, Richard US flyer who, with Calin Rossetti, made the first single-engined flight around the world over the poles in 1987.

Oliver The so-called 'Flying Monk of Malmesbury', said to have leaped from the Abbey Tower wearing wings in 1020. Broke his leg.

Pangborn, Clyde US flyer, with Hugh Herndon, flew non-stop across the Pacific, from Japan to the USA (7300 km) in 1931.

US pilot Wiley Post's long-distance feats are recorded on the side of the Winnie Mae.

□ INDEX □

Penaud, Alphonse Built first elastic-driven propeller model aeroplane (1871).

Peltier, Therese First woman to fly in an aeroplane (as a passenger) in 1908 when she went aloft with Leon Delagrange in his Voisin biplane.

Post, Wiley US flyer who with Harold Gatty flew around the world in 1931. In 1933 became the first solo pilot to circle the globe.

Quimby, Harriet US flyer, first woman pilot to fly the English Channel (1912).

Rodgers, Calbraith Perry US flyer, first pilot to cross the USA from east to west (1911).

Santos-Dumont, Alberto Brazilian flyer who experimented with airships and in 1906 made the first aeroplane flight in Europe.

Scott, Sheila British flyer, the first European woman to fly solo around the world (1966). In 1971 she made the first solo flight in a light plane over the North Pole. She died in 1988.

Selfridge, William First person to die in an aeroplane crash (17 September 1908).

Smith, Elinor American pilot who, at the age of 17, set an endurance record in 1929 by flying for almost 26½ hours. At 15 she had her flying licence suspended for flying beneath the East River bridges in Manhattan.

Smith, Keith and Ross Australian brothers, flew from Britain to Australia in 1919 (27 days 20 hours overall, including stops).

Solar Challenger First man-powered aeroplane to fly the English Channel, piloted by Paul MacCready (1981).

Warsitz, Erich German pilot of the world's first jet plane, the He 178 (27 August 1939).

Whitehead, Gustav German pioneer, working in the USA, who is said to have flown before the Wrights, in 1901.

Wright, Wilbur and Orville Constructed first aeroplane, *Flyer No 1*, to achieve powered, man-carrying flight, covering a distance of 36.5 metres (1903).

Yeager, Charles First person to fly supersonically, in the Bell X-1 rocket plane (1947).

Zambeccarri, Count Italian balloonist who lost several fingers from frostbite when flying at high altitude and died in 1812 when his combination balloon caught fire. He jumped from the basket at tree-top height, but was killed by the fall.

1
17

17

18

18

18

189

190
190

190

191

192

192

1939
1947

1949

1969

1978

1981
1986

hc

Feelings

Caring

Sarah Medina

Illustrated by Jo Brooker

Raintree

www.raintreepublishers.co.uk
Visit our website to find out more information about **Raintree** books.

To order:
 Phone 44 (0) 1865 888112
Send a fax to 44 (0) 1865 314091
Visit the Raintree Bookshop at **www.raintreepublishers.co.uk** to browse our catalogue and order online.

First published in Great Britain by Raintree,
Halley Court, Jordan Hill, Oxford OX2 8EJ,
part of Harcourt Education.
Raintree is a registered trademark of
Harcourt Education Ltd.

Editorial: Dan Nunn, Cassie Mayer and
  Diyan Leake
Design: Joanna Hinton-Malivoire and
  Ron Kamen
Picture research: Erica Newbery
Illustration: Jo Brooker
Production: Duncan Gilbert

Originated by Modern Age
Printed and bound in China by
  South China Printing Company

ISBN 978 1 4062 0638 8
11 10 09 08 07
10 9 8 7 6 5 4 3 2 1

British Library Cataloguing in Publication Data
Medina, Sarah
Feelings: Caring
152.4'1

A full catalogue record for this book is available
from the British Library.

Acknowledgements
The publishers would like to thank the following
for permission to reproduce photographs:
Bananastock p. **22A**, **B**, D; Getty Images/Taxi
p. **22C**; Getty Images/photodisc p. **6**, **7**.

Every effort has been made to contact copyright
holders of any material reproduced in this book.
Any omissions will be rectified in subsequent
printings if notice is given to the publishers.

Contents

Some words are shown in bold, **like this**. They are explained in the glossary on page 23.

What does caring mean?

When you have different feelings, you do or say different things. Caring is like a **feeling**.

proud

angry

sad

4

When you are caring, you think of how others feel. You do nice things for people.

What happens when I am caring?

When you are caring, you want to be kind to other people.

6

You think about how you can help them.

Is it easy to be caring?

Being caring is great, but it is not always easy! Sometimes you have to remember to be caring.

Think about how nice it feels when someone is caring. Then decide how you can be caring, too.

How can I be caring?

You can be caring in lots of ways. You can help to make breakfast or clean the house.

You can remember to say, "Please" and "Thank you". Try to say something nice to someone every day.

13

Are people always caring?

Sometimes people forget to be caring. They might be too busy.

Be caring to them, anyway. Then they might remember that being caring is best!

Can I help someone to be caring?

If someone is not caring, show them what to do. Think of ways you can be caring together.

If your *baby brother* is asleep, you
can play quietly so you do not wake
him up.

17

What should I do when someone is caring?

When someone is caring to you, tell them how great it feels. Say a big "Thank you!"

Do something nice for them another time. Then they will know that you care about them, too.

Enjoy being caring!

Being caring is wonderful! It makes other people feel good. It makes you feel great, too.

If someone is caring, be happy. Then pass on the good **feeling**. Be caring to someone else!

What are these feelings?

A

B

C

D

Which of these people look happy?
What are the other people feeling?
Look at page 24 to see the answers.

Picture glossary

feeling
something that you feel
inside. Caring is like
a feeling.

notice
see

Index

Answers to the questions on page 22

The person in picture C looks happy. The other people could be sad, angry, or jealous.

Note to Parents and Teachers

Reading for information is an important part of a child's literacy development. Learning begins with a question about something. Help children think of themselves as investigators and researchers by encouraging their questions about the world around them. Most chapters in this book begin with a question. Read the question together. Look at the pictures. Talk about what you think the answer might be. Then read the text to find out if your predictions were correct. Think of other questions you could ask about the topic, and discuss where you might find the answers. Assist children in using the picture glossary and the index to practice new vocabulary and research skills.

Titles in the *Feelings* series include:

Hardback 978 1 4062 0634 0

Hardback 978 1 4062 0638 8

Hardback 978 1 4062 0635 7

Hardback 978 1 4062 0637 1

Hardback 978 1 4062 0639 5

Hardback 978 1 4062 0636 4

Find out about the other titles from Raintree on our website www.raintreepublishers.co.uk